WINDSURFING RACE TACTICS

WINDSURFING RACE TACTICS

Noel Swanson

STANFORD MARITIME
LONDON

Stanford Maritime Limited
Member Company of the George Philip Group
12–14 Long Acre   London WC2E 9LP
Editor Phoebe Mason

First published in Great Britain 1985
Copyright © Noel Swanson 1985

Set in 10/11 pt Melior
by Tameside Filmsetting Limited
Ashton-under-Lyne, Lancashire
Diagrams by the Author
Printed in Great Britain by
BAS Printers Limited
Over Wallop, Hampshire

British Library Cataloguing in Publication Data

Swanson, Noel
    Windsurfing Race Tactics.
    1. Windsurfing
    I. Title
    797.3'3   GV811.63.W56

ISBN 0-540-07281-8

To Karen,
With Love

Contents

Preface

In this book I have tried to analyse most of the situations that will occur in windsurfing races. Each section starts with a particular situation and then examines the possibilities open to each of the boards involved. It then follows through these various possibilities to see how Black may defend herself against White's tactics and *vice versa*. Often the section will come to no definite conclusion since in many cases either, or any, of the boards may come out ahead, depending on who uses her tactics most effectively, indeed it is surprising how often a seemingly disastrous position may be turned to advantage by a knowledge of the Racing Rules and how to use them.

A good understanding of the Racing Rules is, of course, essential, and it is expected that the reader will have a copy of them to hand. As well as knowing the Rules, anyone who wishes to race seriously must be confident of his board handling. Knowing the correct tactic for every situation will not win you a race unless you have the ability to carry it out under any circumstances.

Although I have covered as many positions as I could think of, there are no doubt many others that may occur during actual racing. Many of these on analysis turn out to be a combination of two or three of the situations described in this book, and the reader will have little difficulty in extrapolating the tactics covered here to his own situation. If there are any glaring omissions, or any inconsistencies or mistakes, I would be pleased to hear about them so that the next edition may be corrected.

Finally, throughout the book I have referred to the boards as 'she' and 'her'. This is simply in deference to the age-old tradition that yachts are of the female gender, and it is in no way meant to liken the characteristics of sailboards to the females of our species.

Noel Swanson

1
Winning

The object of racing is to win, and doing so requires not just good board handling and tactics but also adequate preparation: many races have been lost through preventable gear failure, forgotten safety tallies, and the many other symptoms of poor preparation.

Racing is held at all levels. Many people are happy to compete at a club level and might make winning the club series their goal for the season. Others are prepared to put more training, more time, and more money into their sport in order to try to compete at a national or even international level. Whatever the level you choose to race at, it is important to have a goal, and to know what that goal is, in order to have any chance of winning consistently. For the club sailor it may just be 'to win the series'; for the more serious competitor the goal must be much more specific, and should include not just the final event to be won, but also the level of success and the events to be sailed in the period leading up to the final competition. An example of a programme for an Olympic aspirant is shown in Appendix 3. Having formulated a programme, you can then adapt your training around it, so avoiding the problems of peaking too soon and of losing enthusiasm because of training too hard, too soon.

Improving technique is the main aim of the training program, and is well covered in a number of excellent books. Also of great importance is fitness, and this should go hand in hand with the improvement of technique. It is also outside of the scope of this book, but a suitable training scheme for the club sailor, that can be done easily at home, is included in Appendix 2.

Having decided, then, which events to attend, we will now cover some of the preparation for each one.

Time and Place Whatever the event, whether a World Championship or a Wednesday evening club race, it is vital to know when and where it is being held. Having found out, make sure that you arrive in plenty of time – days for an international event, perhaps an hour for a race at your club. This will give you enough time to check everything, and also to get to know the area if it is foreign to you.

Event Formalities Having arrived suitably early, find out about the registration formalities; whether boards and sails will be measured and where; and whether personal weight will be checked. Read the Sailing Instructions and find out about any tally system that is being used.

Towards the end of the series, check on your own and your main opponents' points before each race to see if they will influence your tactics.

Gear Before every race quickly check all your equipment, and replace any broken parts. Check also that the various pieces of rope are not about to wear right through. Choose the correct equipment for the expected conditions.

Psychological Warfare Unfortunately, this occurs to a great extent in the higher levels of racing. Also known as 'psyching someone out', it consists of using direct or indirect ways of decreasing an opponent's morale and decreasing their estimate of their rightful finishing place. It is very difficult to overtake someone if you are convinced that they are faster than you and that they 'belong' ahead of you. There are many methods in use, some deliberate and many on a sub-conscious level. For example, many people are insecure in their choice of equipment and can easily be persuaded that theirs is not the fastest sail around.

The only defence to these pressures is to be well prepared, and to know that you are well prepared. You can then look on in amusement at those less prepared than yourself who are getting very worked up about which sail to use or whether they will get on the water in time for the start.

2
The Start

The start is often cited as the most crucial part of the race, and indeed a good start lets you sail the first leg in clear air, with few boards getting in the way, and with confidence; while a bad starts puts you in dirty wind, amidst a mass of poorly handled boards, and is demoralising. A bad start means that to win you must first catch up and then overtake the leaders, whereas a good start means that you have but to sail the same speed as the others in order to keep the lead.

So a good start is vital. It is also difficult to achieve unless practised often, and it needs a lot of concentration, good board handling and confidence to get it right.

2.1 STARTING TO WINDWARD

This is by far the most common type of start, and also the fairest since it offers every board the chance of clean air. It also means that the fleet will be spread out by the time the leaders reach the first mark, so preventing the confusion of too many boards trying to round at the same time. There are two varieties of windward start, the **gate start** and the **line start**. The line start is more commonly used for large fleets and is the one we shall consider first.

2.11 Line Starts
2.111 Which end?
A good start consists of being on the line at the

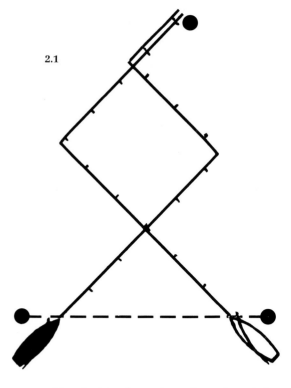

2.1

gun, sailing fast in clean air, and starting at the right end of the line. So clearly the first thing to be decided is which end of the line to start at. If the line is placed at right angles to the wind, then

2.2

2.3

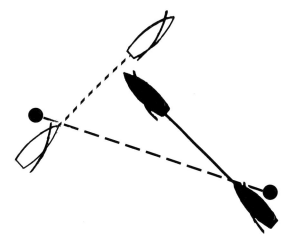

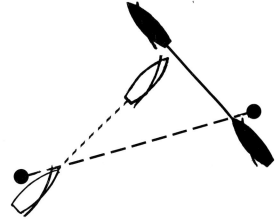

White who starts at the port end will reach the windward mark at the same time as Black who starts at the starboard end (2.1). This line is therefore not biased to either end, and a board that starts well at any point along the line will do as well as anyone else.

However, a line is rarely so well laid, and usually it will be biased to one end or the other. In the case of (2.2) the port end of the line is slightly closer to the windward mark than the starboard end, and we can see that although they both start at the same time, White crosses ahead of Black by a considerable distance. Similarly, if the starboard end is farther upwind (2.3) then it becomes the favoured end, and this time it is Black who comes out in the lead when both sail at the same angle to the wind.

So it follows that we want to start at the favoured end if there is one. As soon as the line has been laid, therefore, we set about determin-

ing the favoured end. The most accurate way to do this is to wait at one end of the line, and then when someone else does a practice start at the other end we also cross the line. Fairly soon, we shall see who is ahead, and so who has the favoured end.

Another method is to cross the line yourself first on one tack and then on the other (2.4). As

2.4

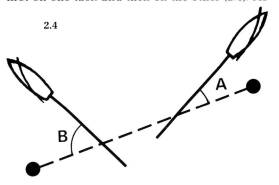

13

you cross, estimate whether the angle A is greater or less than 45°. If the starboard end is favoured angle A will be less than 45°, and angle B will be greater than 45°. Conversely, if the port end is favoured then angle B will be less than angle A.

This method is not as accurate as the first, but it will quickly show up lines that are very biased: sometimes the bias is so great that on one tack you are sailing almost parallel to the line, and on the other tack at right angles to it. In (2.5) it is the port end that is so heavily favoured: White can only just cross the line on starboard.

2.5

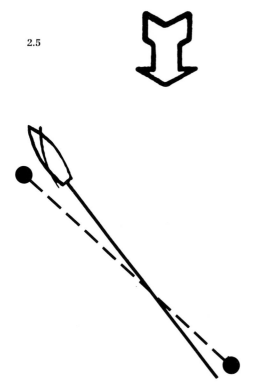

This method can be made more accurate by starting first at the starboard end on starboard tack, and then at the port end on port (2.6). White sails far enough on each tack so that she can estimate the distance to the end of the line when

it is at right angles to her. The two distances AB and BC are then compared, and the shorter one indicates the favoured end, in this case C.

A third method is to sail up and down along the line itself (2.7). In each direction White notes whether she is on a beam reach, close fetch or whatever. If the line is biased, she will be sailing farther off the wind when going away from the favoured end. Here, she is on a beam reach on starboard tack and on a close fetch on port, and so the starboard end is again favoured.

One or two of these methods should be used several times before the start to determine which is the favoured end, and then to make sure that the marks are not dragging or the wind shifting, so that the favoured end could change before the race actually starts. Having done that, we can then concentrate on getting into position for the start.

Finally, having decided on the favoured end, we might (unusually) decide to start at the 'wrong' end because it offers significant advantages with respect to our strategy for the beat to the first mark (covered in Chapter 3).

Tide

If the line is laid across water where the tidal stream flows uniformly, then it makes absolutely no difference to the decision of which end to start at. It is a fallacy to think that the end which is farther uptide is favoured.

In (2.8), Black and White start at the same time at opposite ends of the line. It is at right angles to the wind, but the starboard end is farther uptide. Their courses are shown both as they would be *without* any tide (broken line) and when the effects of the tide are taken into account (solid). White sails forward 400m and drifts 100m sideways, while Black sails forward 400m and drifts backwards 100m also. As we can see, both boards are still level, as they would have been if there were no tide.

On the other hand, if the line is laid near the shore or partly over shallows, then the variation in the strength of the tide does need to be

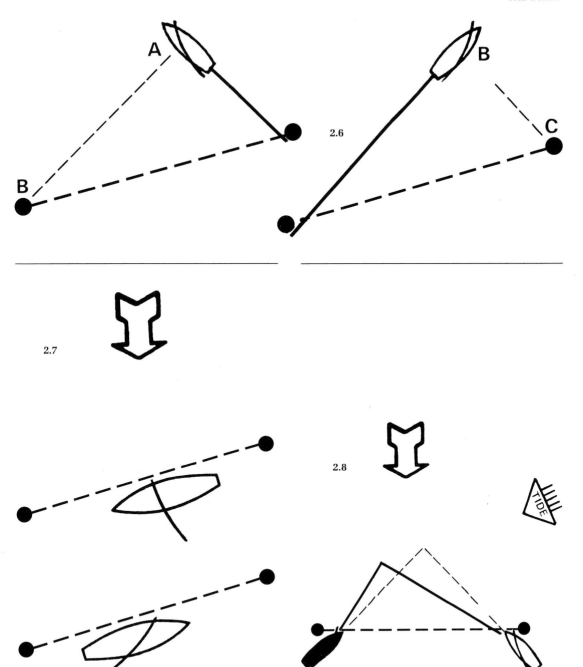

2.6

2.7

2.8

TIDE

considered (2.9). Here the line is laid close to the shore, and of course the tide is weaker in the shallows than out in the channel. The line is set at right angles to the wind. White sets off from the starboard (shore) end, sailing against a weak tide, while Black sets off at the same time from the port end which is out in the stronger stream. Their courses as affected by the tide are shown, and White crosses clear ahead of Black. Had the tide been flowing in the opposite direction, then Black would have come out ahead, since the stronger stream would have been in a favourable direction.

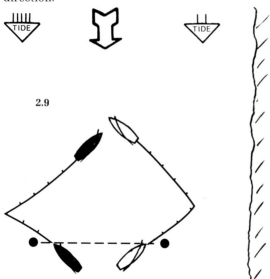

2.9

When the tide varies across the line, and the line is also biased with respect to the wind, it can be very difficult to decide at which end to start. The only way of telling is by a trial start, setting off at one end while someone else sets off from the other end as described above.

2.112 Starting in large fleets

There are a number of points that make starting in very large fleets (thirty boards or more) different from smaller club fleets. First of all is the phenomenon of the line bulge. While boards at the ends of the line can easily see when they are over the line, those towards the middle are not quite certain where the line is (2.10). Furthermore, since there is a board on each side of her White reasons that even if she is slightly over the line, the committee boat cannot see her sail number and so she cannot be disqualified. The others also reason in the same way, and so *en masse* they all edge over the line, each making sure that there is someone on either side so that she cannot be seen by the committee boat. In this way it is not unusual for eighty per cent of the fleet to be premature starters. Of course this usually results in a general recall. However, occasionally such a start is allowed to go ahead, and when it does then White clearly has made an excellent start.

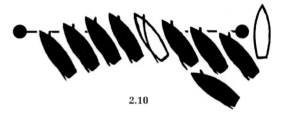

2.10

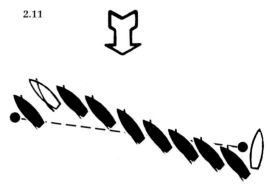

2.11

When the line is fair the maximum point of the bulge is at the centre, but when the line is biased the bulge moves closer to the favoured end (2.11). Often the line is biased to port and the committee boat is moored at the starboard end. In these cases the port end of the line may be totally ignored as a one-sided bulge forms. Again, no one is identifiable since they all have someone shielding them from view. Tactics in a large fleet are therefore to be at the front of the bulge, but out of view, and to be there for every single start and re-start, since it is always the start where one is not in the bulge that is allowed to continue!

When the stream is flowing against the wind, the bulge may become particularly severe (2.12) as everyone gets pushed over the line by the water as well as by the normal process of the bulge. It is in this sort of situation that race officers have been known *not* to call a general recall, but rather to disqualify *everyone* except those few whom they could positively identify as not being over the line.

After a general recall race officers often decide to invoke the five-minute rule: that anyone over the line *at any time* in the five minutes before the start will be disqualified. This often, and understandably, results in intense line-shyness, with no one coming anywhere near the line lest they be disqualified for being over it. The result of this is a line sag (2.13). Again, those at the ends of the line know where they are. But towards the middle nobody is quite sure and all assume that their neighbour is approximately on it. And again, everyone makes sure that *he* cannot be seen by the committee boat. Even so, they are scared of being over the line and so the line sags away at the middle.

The answer to this one is to know where the line is, accurately (2.14). With this knowledge, and confidence, White starts on the line at the gun or even half a length behind it for safety, and yet is 30m ahead of the rest of the fleet. Line sag is also made worse by any stream, this time when it is in the same direction as the wind, making it difficult to sail up to the line.

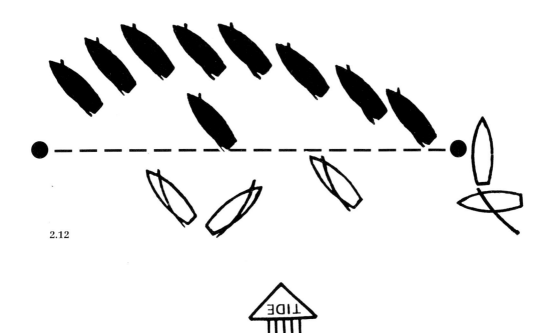

2.12

17

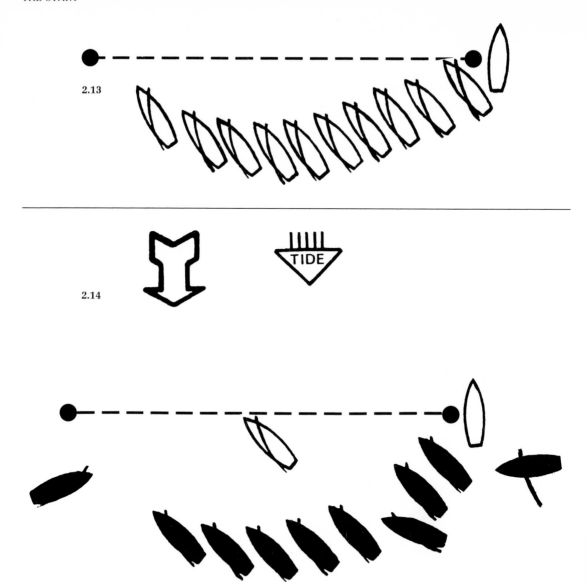

2.13

2.14

TIDE

2.113 Getting to the line

During the five minutes after the ten-minute gun, we will have decided which end of the line is favoured and whether there are any particular reasons, such as variations in the tide, as to why we should not start there. We will also have considered whether or not there is likely to be a bulge or sag, and whereabouts the maximum point will be. Having weighed up all these factors, we come to a decision on where on the line to start. The final piece of information needed is where the line is.

As we saw in relation to line sag, accurately locating the line can win races. The best way to do it is by lining it up with a transit on shore (2.15). White does this by going to the offshore end of the line, looking back along it and finding a landmark that is directly in line with the far end. She then knows that whenever she sees the inshore end mark in transit with the landmark, she is on the line.

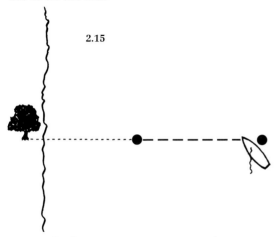

2.15

Near the five-minute gun we stop what we are doing and check our watch, counting down to the gun. If the gun is on time, good. If not, then we can mentally correct the watch so that we will start on time.

It is now time to start positioning for the start. Tactics are the same for large and small fleets, but obviously it is much easier to start on an empty line than a crowded one. During the final two minutes a solid wall of boards builds up on the line. Anyone arriving later will be unable to get through it to the line, and so will have a disastrous start. Therefore the principle is to arrive at the chosen spot on the line, in clean air, and with plenty of space to leeward so that we can free off and power out of the start.

Unfortunately, good starting cannot be learned instantly from principles: it needs constant practice to apply them properly.

Starboard end start

In a small fleet White aims to start right next to the mark. After the five-minute gun she does a practice start, sailing up to the starboard end closehauled at about half speed and noting about how long it takes for the approach. If necessary, she then repeats this until she is confident of being able to cross the line on time in the right place.

At the appropriate time she commences the real run-up. By sailing at sub-maximum speed she can adjust her approach to arrive with perfect timing. If any boards try to barge in between her and the starboard end mark White tells them to keep clear (2.16). It is important to

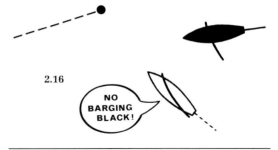

2.16

NO BARGING BLACK!

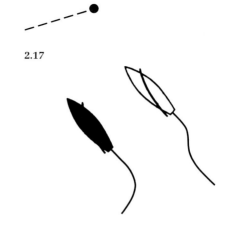

2.17

keep plenty of room to leeward, so if anyone sails up under her White luffs up slightly to give herself some more room (2.17).

She arrives about 5m short of the line and waits there with her sail flapping until about 10–15 seconds before the gun (2.18). White then sheets in, bears away slightly, and accelerates to maximum speed to cross the line with the gun (2.19). She has started perfectly, at the correct end of the line and in clean air.

In large fleets the above starting method needs slight modification (2.20). First of all, White must arrive at the hover position at least two minutes before the gun, otherwise she will be unable to fight her way through the crowd of boards to get to the front line, like Grey in this example. Retaining that position then requires plenty of confidence: White must not be afraid of staying in the front line, even if a bulge forms and she starts getting pushed over before the start (2.21).

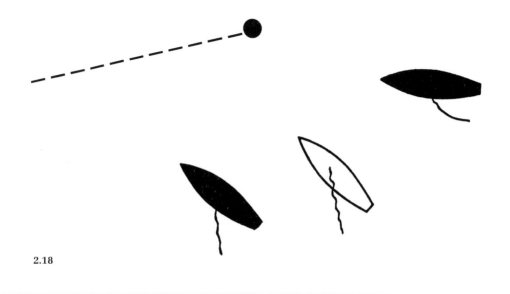

2.18

2.19

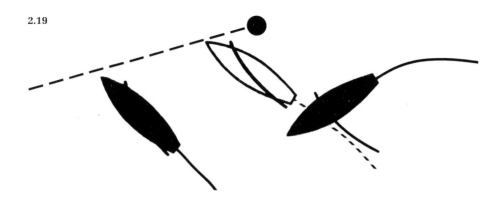

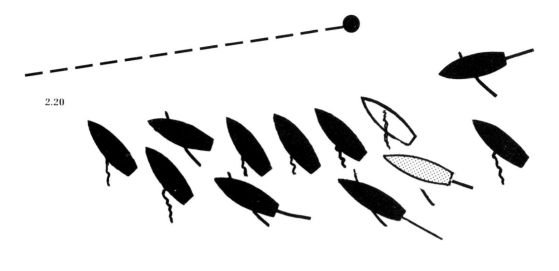

2.20

2.21

Secondly, in large fleets there is nearly always a large number of boards all trying to get the prime position, right next to the mark at the favoured end (2.22). Needless to say only one board actually succeeds, in this case Grey, and all the others make only second-rate starts.

White decides to avoid all this confusion and aims to start *near* the favoured end but not actually *at* it (2.23). In this way she can assure herself of a good start, and although she may be a few feet behind Grey because of the line bias she is certainly much better off than all the others.

Starting in the middle of the line, or at the port end

Tactics for starting at the middle of the line are the same as those for the port end.

In small fleets White approaches the line in the same way as for the starboard end, but instead of sailing closehauled she sails on a close fetch (2.24). By doing this she can weave around any boards ahead and also alter her speed at the same time so that she can put herself near the line with plenty of space to leeward. When she

2.22

2.23

2.24

has to overtake someone to get to the line she tends to go to leeward of them since she can then keep a space to leeward. Again, she waits just before the line until ten seconds to go, and then sheets in and accelerates for the gun.

In large fleets what usually happens is that a large number of boards congregate near the starboard end of the line and then in the last minute they reach down it towards the port end until the gun goes, at which point they harden up to closehauled. Since all these boards must give way to any boards to leeward of them they are often forced over the line, resulting in a port end bulge.

White adapts her tactics to this. She approaches the line as before, but aiming for a point nearer the starboard end than she wishes to start. She must get there at least one minute early, and aims to be to leeward of the mob (2.25). As she approaches the position she luffs anyone to windward of her so that she creates a gap to leeward.

As the rush begins, White makes sure that she is hovering on the line so that anybody who tries to sail over her must be across the line. Inevitably, as the boards sail down the line to the port end some of them will pass behind White, and like G1 will probably find that they cannot get back into clean air.

Others will try to sail over White, like G2. White shouts 'Windward boards keep clear – Up!' White can then bear away and sail a bit farther down the line, using the gap that she made for herself, in order to stay in clean wind.

If large numbers of boards are forced over the line (2.27), then White will also have to sail forward with them in order to stay in the front row and in undisturbed wind. It will probably result in a general recall, but if not White must be up with them to have any hope of a good start.

The port tack start

The object of a port tack start is to cross the line at the port end, when it is heavily favoured, and then to sail across the front of the whole fleet tacking to windward of it to consolidate the lead (2.28).

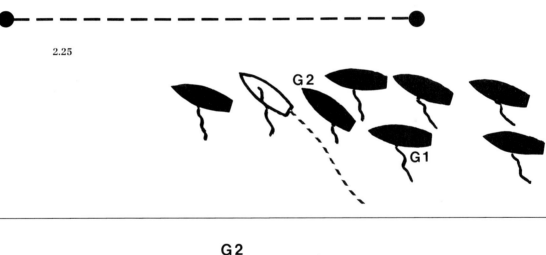

2.25

2.26

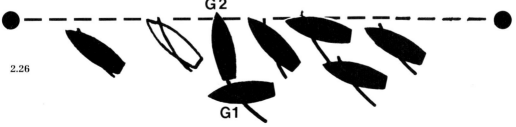

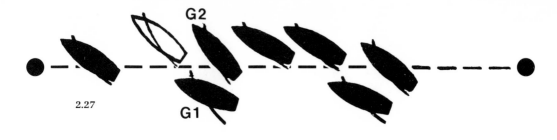

2.27

G2

G1

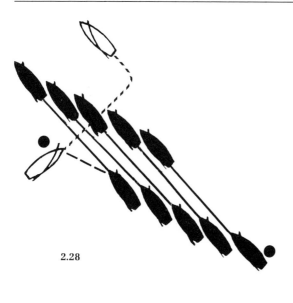

2.28

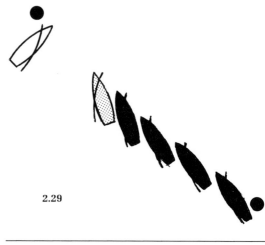

2.29

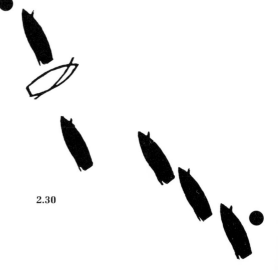

2.30

However, except when the line is so biased that it can hardly be crossed on starboard tack, this is a very risky tactic and should be avoided. When the line is so biased, there is often a gap between the leading board on starboard (Grey) and the port mark (2.29). White slips through this gap on port tack. She must time it perfectly since if she is late she will have to give way to all the starboard tack boards.

If she cannot start right next to the mark she will often be able to slip through between two starboard tack boards (2.30). If this comes off she will have made a better start than all of them.

The dip start

This tactic is particularly useful when there is a strong stream running with the wind, making it very difficult to maintain a hovering position on the line. It cannot be used when the Five or One Minute Rules are in operation, and it is more difficult to use when the line is heavily biased since it will be difficult to start at the favoured end.

White stays to windward of the line (2.31). In the last minute before the start she looks along it for a suitable gap between the boards that are approaching the line. If the stream is with the wind the line may well sag, making this easy.

White swoops down from the wrong side of the line 30 seconds before the start (2.32) and then luffs up to start at full speed on the gun, while the rest of the fleet are still struggling to

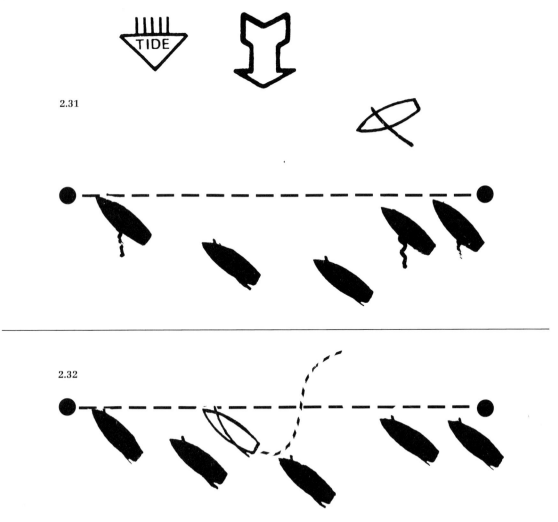

2.31

2.32

sail up to the line against the stream. Needless to say, White must make sure that she is fully on the right side of the line before the gun goes off.

2.114 After the start

At the gun White is in her chosen position on the line and travelling at maximum speed. The first few minutes after the gun are crucial: White ignores all those around her, ignores wind shifts and her strategy for the beat, and simply concentrates entirely on speed for about five minutes. She makes sure that she is sailing free and not pinching, and works hard at squeezing the last tenth of a knot from the board. After about five minutes White should be ahead in clean air. Only then can she look around, evaluate her position and consider her strategy. If she does not concentrate on maintaining maximum speed she will end up in dirty wind as those above her sail right over her.

If White has made a bad start, then her first priority is to stay calm. Swearing will only slow her down. She then devotes herself to finding clean wind and to carrying out her general strategy for the beat. If she thinks positively and believes that her rightful place *is* at the front, then there is no reason that she cannot work her way up the fleet. If she thinks 'Typical .... start!' then she is very likely to stay in the middle of the fleet.

2.115 Tactics with one opponent

Occasionally White may have only one opponent whom she needs to beat. This occurs most obviously in match racing, but also at the end of a series when the points are such that White *must* beat Black, whatever position they both end up in, in order to win the series. These tactics are also particularly useful in team racing.

In any of these circumstances the match between Black and White starts at the five-minute gun, when the Racing Rules take effect. White aims to keep herself between the line and Black, so that she will always have the better start. She does this by following close behind Black wherever she goes.

Here Black is sailing on a reach, looking at the line (2.33). White joins her and tags onto her stern. (For the purpose of this discussion we shall ignore the rest of the fleet.) Black realizes she is being followed and tries to break free by luffing. White also luffs, staying upwind of her.

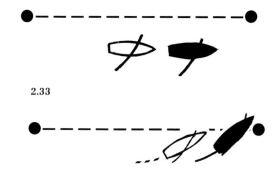

2.33

Black cannot tack because of White's position, and if she carries on she will obviously be sailing away from the line and so is bound to start late. So Black bears away again and White follows suit (2.34). As Black gybes White also gybes, and again stays upwind of Black.

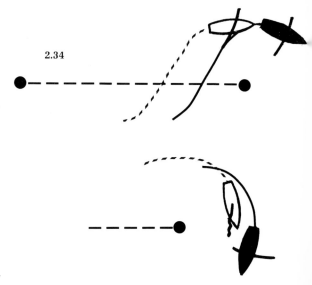

2.34

Again Black is being sailed away from the line, and so she luffs up to closehauled on starboard (2.35). Because she sails a tighter turn White ends up slightly ahead, and if the starting gun has already fired she will go for the line to start ahead of Black. If the gun has not gone, Black may try to tack beneath White to break cover.

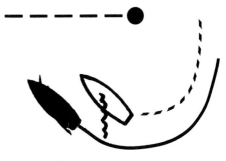

2.36

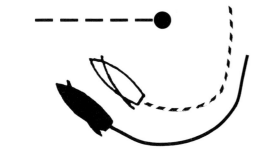

2.35

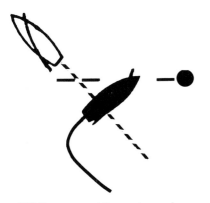

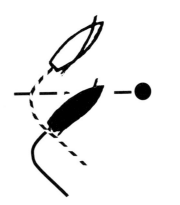

White can either slow down slightly to prevent this (2.36), or she may herself tack to cover again.

Black's only hope of starting ahead of White is to break her cover somehow. This is usually achieved by doing a succession of fast turns, gybes, and tacks to try to catch White out. However, if White is skillful she should be able to prevent Black from ever breaking free. This manoeuvring will continue until after the start, when White decides to break off and sail for the

line knowing that she will start ahead of Black and in a position to cover her.

Usually there will also be other boards about, and in that case Black will try to use the presence of another racer to break White's grip. In (2.37) Black calls on White for room to tack for a board on starboard. Once she has tacked, Black is to windward of White, the roles have been reversed, and Black can now tail White rather than the other way round. Now it is Black that will start ahead.

2.2 GATE STARTS

The alternative method for starting races to windward is the gate start. This is frequently used for club races when there is no race officer to lay a line, but it is also used occasionally in larger meetings. The principle is that one board,

2.37

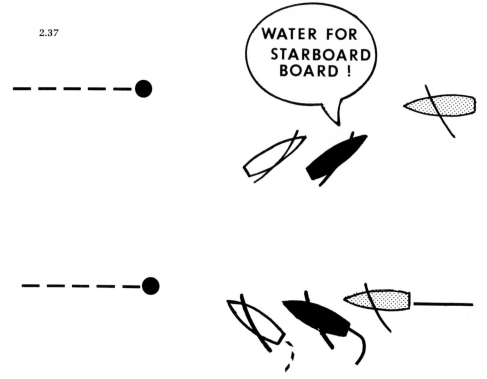

the 'pathfinder', sails on port tack past a single buoy which then marks the port end of the gate. The rest of the fleet, on starboard tack, then start at any time they like between the buoy and the stern of the pathfinder. Everyone who starts immediately under his stern makes a perfect start, and all those who make a perfect start are then level with each other, whether they start early (A) or late (B). Those who do not start immediately below the pathfinder, such as C, have started badly (2.38).

Once everyone has started, the pathfinder is free to tack off himself. To make the system work the pathfinder is protected and it is an infringement of the rules to collide or interfere with him while he is opening the gate. Gate starts make starting well very easy: White merely waits for the pathfinder to reach her and then she sheets in and sails through the gate.

Since nearly everyone starts perfectly, though, how does one gain maximum benefit from a gate start? The best way to look at a gate start is to consider the race as starting at the port end mark. What is the correct course to sail from there at the time that the pathfinder passes? This question is answered with regard to the strategy for the first beat (see next Chapter), and with reference to the wind shifts – will port or starboard get a lift?

Having considered these points White can then decide whether to start early or late. If she considers that starboard tack and/or the port hand side of the course is favoured, then she will start early. On the other hand, if port tack, or the starboard side of the course, is favoured, then White lets the pathfinder sail that tack for her and starts late. She then has room to tack onto port herself if she wishes to do so.

PATHFINDER

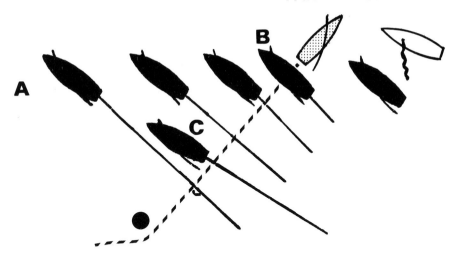

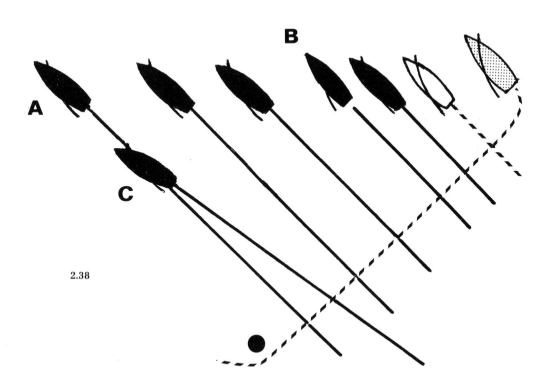

2.38

2.3 REACHING AND RUNNING STARTS

Reaching and running starts (2.39) are fairly uncommon since they are not nearly as effective as windward starts in spreading the fleet out and so avoiding congestion at the first mark.

Downwind starts are particularly bad in this respect, since the leaders are continually blanketed by those behind them. The result is that they all arrive at the first mark as one mob.

2.39

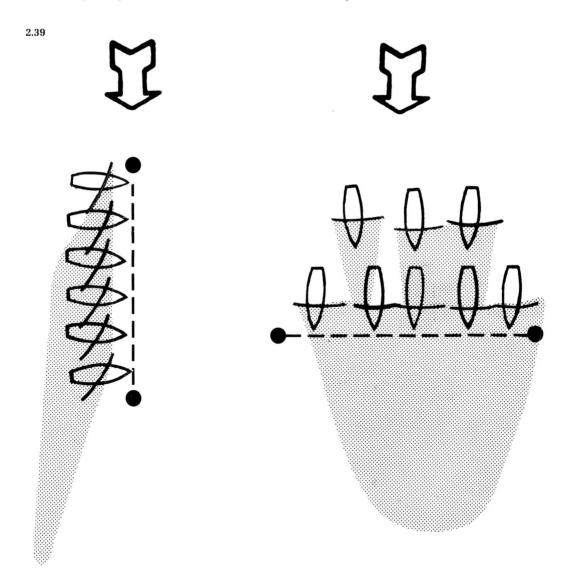

Reaching starts

The first point to consider when starting on a reach is which end is nearer to the first mark. In this case (2.40) the port end P is clearly much nearer the first mark M than is S. And so, all things being equal, this would be the correct end at which to start. However, the other important consideration is to have undisturbed wind for the reach, and for this the windward end is clearly favoured.

The fairest line, therefore, is one that has the leeward end nearer the mark (W-L). Thus boards starting to windward have the advantage of clear air, while those to leeward have less distance to sail. In practice, the most important point is clean wind, and this applies especially in

2.40

marginal conditions where it may make the difference between planing or displacement sailing.

Starting tactics are similar to those for a beat; on crowded lines a wall will build up and so a hover start is most appropriate – choosing the place to start and sitting there until just before the gun and then accelerating for the line. After crossing the main considerations are again board speed and clean air, trying to get onto the plane and staying there.

Running starts

These are very difficult to do well. The aim is to start right at one end of the line so that straight afterwards one can sail over to that side of the course to find clean air. The end to choose really depends on the side to which the first mark is to be taken, and the tactics are those for any run (see Chapter 9).

STARTING CHECKLIST

ON SHORE

Check Forecast —Any expected changes in wind direction or strength?

Check Tide —Direction, strength, any expected changes?

Check Equipment —Everything working, correct sail for conditions?

Check Sailing Instructions —The course, and methods for changing or shortening it? Any five or one minute rules?

Check Points —Any particular opponent to be beaten?

Collect Tally if necessary.

ON THE WATER
Practise a few tacks and gybes to loosen up.
Sail a practice first beat if possible.
Decide on strategy for the first beat.

Ten Minute Gun
Start watch
Check line: which end is favoured?

Practise start
Check line again: any change?
Wait for five minute gun

Five Minute Gun
Check watch
Check line for last time

Three Minutes
Start run-up to chosen starting point

Two Minutes
Should now be taking up position in front row of the wall, but still back from the line. Make sure there is room to leeward.

One Minute
Now near the line, make room to leeward. Stay with the bulge if it forms.

Thirty Seconds
Start sheeting in, edging forward

Fifteen Seconds
Accelerate to maximum speed. Free off.

START
Keep cool
Sail fast and don't pinch
Ignore everything else for five minutes
Clear air if necessary

Five Minutes After
Evaluate position and follow strategy

General Recall
Keep sailing. Do not return to the line until either you have seen the Recall flag or until a rescue boat crosses ahead of the fleet telling everyone to return. Guns can be fired by mistake!

3
The Beat

3.1 STRATEGY

The beat, especially the first beat, is the leg on which there is the most place-changing. This is because the speed of one board relative to another depends not just on their actual speed through the water but also on a whole host of other factors. It is the sailor who makes the fewest mistakes in negotiating these factors, as well as sailing fast, who will arrive first at the windward mark.

3.11 The Wind

3.111 Predicting wind shifts

It is the differences in atmospheric pressure that cause wind. In general air flows from Highs towards Lows, but because of the earth's rotation (Coriolis Effect) the wind blows parallel to the isobars with the Low pressure to the left of the wind direction (3.1). The greater the difference in pressure (closely spaced isobars as at A) the stronger the winds. On a weather map,

3.1

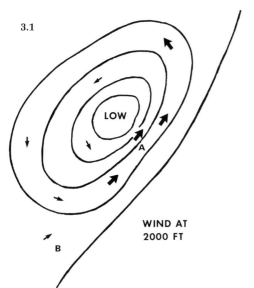

WIND AT
2000 FT

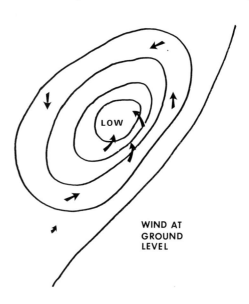

WIND AT
GROUND
LEVEL

33

the direction of the isobars gives the wind direction at about 2000ft up, which is about the altitude of cumulus (cotton wool) clouds. At ground level, however, the wind is slightly deflected and slowed down by friction and so it blows at an angle to the isobars, as shown. Ground level wind is *backed* in relation to the wind moving the clouds, and is not as strong (3.2).

3.2

0 ft

2000 ft

3.112 Exploiting wind shifts

It is changes in wind speed and direction that can be used to improve one's position in a race. Wind never blows uniformly and there are always eddies in it. What happens during a gust is that one of these eddies brings down, as if in a lift, the wind from 2000ft. So for the duration of the eddy we experience the wind from higher altitudes which is both stronger (a gust) and in a different direction (veered). The shift in direction (3.3) is always to the same side (and if in doubt can be checked by looking at the clouds), and results in a lift for White who is on starboard tack, and of course a header for Black on port.

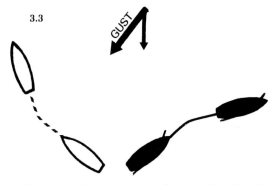

3.3

GUST

Gusts may be seen coming by watching for the darkening of the water, and by looking upwind

to see if the sails ahead get more wind. When a gust is seen to be coming then we have time to tack onto starboard to enjoy the lift that it brings with it.

Rule—A gust means a lift on starboard tack.

On some days, particularly when there are a lot of small, puffy, cumulus clouds (showing the presence of many eddies in the wind), these gusts can be very regular, enabling us to sail the whole beat getting every shift right simply by watching for the gusts.

The aim of the beat is to sail upwind as fast as possible, so White, although she is behind Black, is in fact farther upwind and thus ahead, while Grey is behind both of them. To see who is leading we must draw a line at right angles to the wind for each board, *not* at right angles to their fore-and-aft centrelines (3.4).

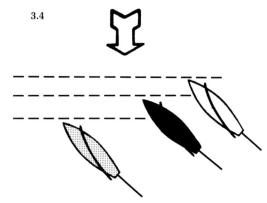

3.4

In (3.5) Black and White are level, and on opposite tacks. The wind is steady, and when they next meet they are still level. However, the wind veers (shifts in a clockwise direction) after they have sailed a short distance (3.6) and White stays on port tack while Black holds on starboard. They alter their courses according to the wind shift and we will now find that White is leading. And indeed, when they both tack next (3.7) we find that White crosses ahead of Black.

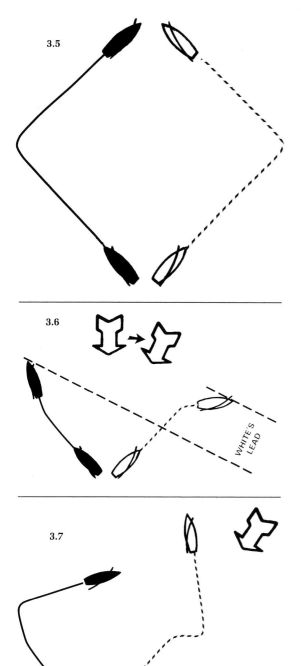

3.5

3.6

WHITE'S LEAD

3.7

So White has benefitted by sailing first on the tack that will be backed when the wind shifts, and then tacking onto the tack that is lifted once the shift has arrived. This gives us our first rule for sailing a beat in shifting winds:

Rule 1—Tack on a backing wind shift.

Look at the same situation, but this time neither board tacks when the wind first veers: instead they carry on until the wind shifts back to its original direction (3.8). We now find that Black is in the lead since she sailed on a lift for a short while, while White, ignoring Rule 1, sailed on a backing windshift.

3.8

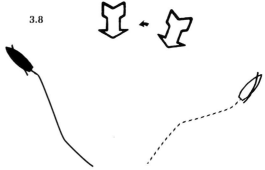

Rule 2—Do not tack on a lift.

Finally, we see what would happen if Black and White both follow the above rules.

The wind veers and so White tacks (3.9). After a while, the wind backs to its original direction again (3.10). This is just a return to the neutral position, not a true backing shift, and so neither board tacks. The boards are still level with each other since they have followed the basic rules for windshifts. As the wind shifts back and forth throughout the beat so Black and White will tack on each backer, the first one to miss one losing the lead. Their course is compared with Grey (3.11), who does just the opposite and tacks on each lift!

3.113 Wind bends

Often, instead of the wind oscillating back and forth as above, it changes steadily in the same

35

3.9

3.10

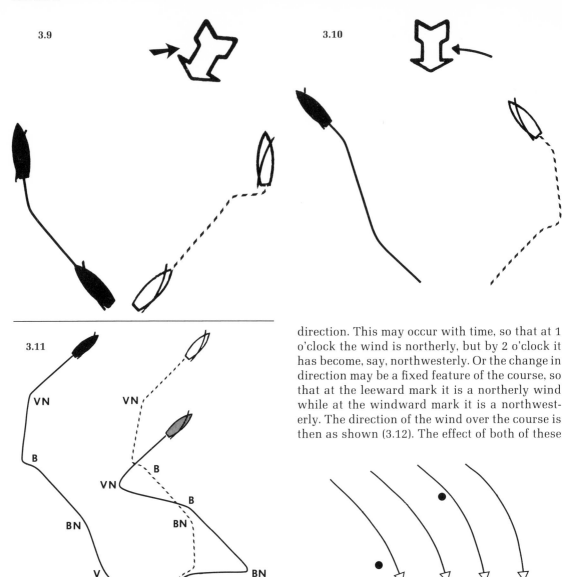

3.11

WIND SHIFTS {
B - Back
BN - Back to neutral
VN - Veer to neutral
V - Veer
}

direction. This may occur with time, so that at 1 o'clock the wind is northerly, but by 2 o'clock it has become, say, northwesterly. Or the change in direction may be a fixed feature of the course, so that at the leeward mark it is a northerly wind while at the windward mark it is a northwesterly. The direction of the wind over the course is then as shown (3.12). The effect of both of these

3.12

is the same, since at the start of the beat (at 1 pm) it is a northerly wind, while at the end of the beat an hour later it is northwesterly. So from the water the two systems are identical and they are both called 'wind bends'.

White and Black are level at the start of the beat (3.13). The wind is not shifting, so they do not tack frequently. White sails off to the port side of the course and Black heads for the starboard side. As they sail along the wind is gradually bending, so Black is lifted while White is headed. The wind continues to change and so the courses they sail are curved.

After a while, but before she reaches the lay line for the mark, White tacks off. She is now on the same tack as Black and so is continually

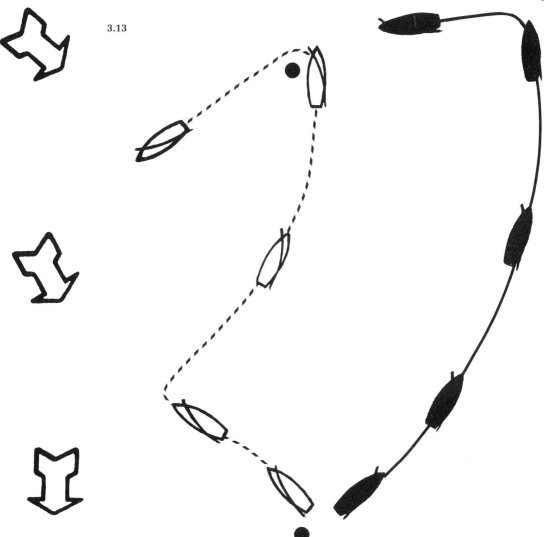

3.13

lifted. Black continues as she was. White now finds that she has been lifted far enough that she can lay the mark.

Black, however, is also lifted, but since she has to tack for the mark she finds herself having to sail far beyond it in order that she may eventually lay it when she does tack. Clearly White has sailed a much shorter course, and is halfway down the reach by the time Black rounds the windward mark.

Rule 3—In a wind bend, sail on the backed tack first, towards the centre of the bend.

Of course wind bends are not always predicted, so what should one do if caught on the wrong side of a bend, as Black was above?

In this case (3.14) Grey starts off by following close on Black's stern. However, after about five minutes she realizes that this lift is not a

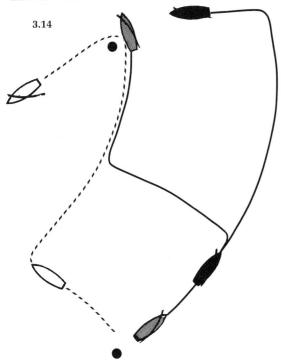

3.14

temporary shift but a permanent bend. So she immediately cuts her losses and tacks off to join White's course as soon as possible. Grey overtakes Black, but does not catch up with White.

Rule 4—If caught on the wrong side of a wind bend, cut your losses and tack off. Do not wait for the wind to shift back – it won't.

Finally, the wind may be shifting on top of an underlying wind bend. In that case the ideal response is to play the shifts as described above, while keeping over to the favoured side of the course to benefit from the wind bend.

Changes in wind direction may be large or small, and may last for a long or short time. In order for it to be worthwhile tacking on a backer the change in direction must be great enough and last long enough for the gain to compensate for the distance lost while tacking. Generally a shift of more than $5°$ is worth tacking on, and this is about the minimum that is detectable when sailing. To see whether a backer will last, it is usually worth sailing through it for a short time, and if it does not revert quickly then tack. It is helpful to watch other boards ahead that also get the shift to see how long it lasts for them. if a shift is particularly large then it is worth tacking immediately, since it will pay off even if it lasts only a short while.

3.114 Predicting wind bends
As we mentioned before, wind bends may be constant features of a course, or they may be due to a gradual and continual change of wind direction with time.

Geographical wind bends occur because of the formation of the land. Wind tends to take the easiest route around obstructions, and so it will be diverted around hills and funnelled down valleys. Here, for instance (3.15), the wind is funnelled down the valley and on reaching the open lake bends back to its original direction. On

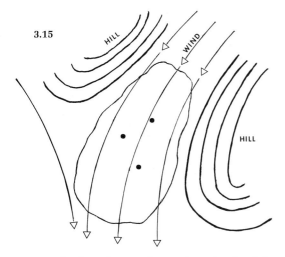

3.15

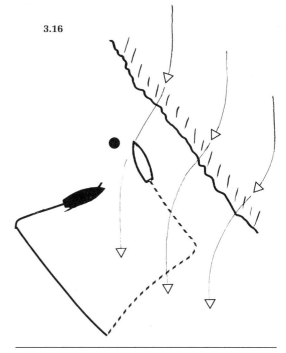

3.16

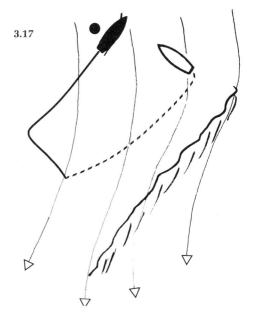

3.17

a course laid as shown, the starboard side of the beat is favoured.

Shore effects Wind will also bend when crossing between land and water. When it blows off the shore on a slant it bends to cross the shoreline at more nearly a right angle, resulting in a wind bend as shown (3.16). Advantage can be taken of this by sailing inshore when beating: White arrives at the mark before Black. When the wind blows at an angle onshore (3.17) it tends to blow more along the shoreline and it then pays to sail out.

Such wind bends can usually be accurately predicted by studying the land before putting the board in the water. Wind bends not caused by land topography can be more difficult to predict. However, there are a few causes that are easily spotted, and interpreting the signs correctly can win races. The first of these is the sea breeze.

The sea breeze occurs only on bright sunny days and happens because land heats up more quickly than water. As the sun shines on the land it heats up. This causes the air over the land to warm up too and it then starts to rise. As it rises it cools and any water vapour condenses to form clouds. The rising air must be replaced by new air coming in at land level (3.18). It comes in from over the sea and is felt as cooler wind blowing onshore, from the sea to the land, and it often reaches a good force 4. As the heated air cools at altitude it is pushed out of the way by more rising air. And the sea breeze coming in must itself be replaced by new air. So a cycle forms, and the heated air cools down and sinks over the sea only to flow back to the land to be heated again. As it blows over the water the sea breeze collects more moisture which then feeds the new clouds over the land, making them grow rapidly. Once this system gets started it spreads

sea breeze sets in there will be a 180° wind shift. This happens fairly rapidly, in perhaps half an hour. Out beyond the sea breeze circulation, the meteorological wind returns (3.19). Similarly, if the wind is along the shore the sea breeze will deflect it more onshore.

Finally, due to the Coriolis effect the sea breeze slowly and persistently veers during the afternoon, so favouring the starboard side of the beating legs.

So, the onset of a sea breeze often causes substantial and rapid wind shifts which can obviously be exploited. It can be predicted:

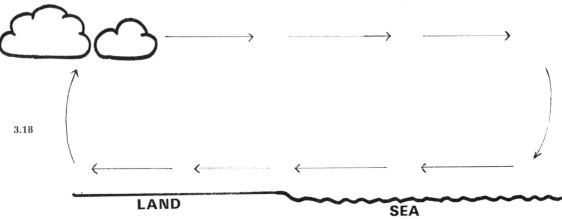

3.18

LAND   SEA

further inland and also farther out to sea.

The sea breeze always blows onshore, so if the prevailing wind on the day is offshore when the

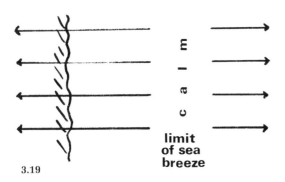

3.19

limit
of sea
breeze

First, by local knowledge. In many places the locals set their watches by the onset of the sea breeze.

Second, by watching for the tell-tale sign of rapidly forming clouds over the land but not over the sea.

Third, by watching sails closer inshore. The breeze starts near the shore and then extends outwards, so those inshore will experience it first.

Frontal systems A front is an area where masses of air at different temperatures meet. Fronts move, and are described as warm or cold depending on the temperature of the air that is arriving.

A cold front occurs when cold air drives under

warm air (3.20). The warm air is pushed up and forms clouds (as with a sea breeze) and these usually result in heavy showers. Cold fronts pass quickly (in a half to one hour) and are accompanied by an increase in wind strength and a *veer* in direction in the Northern Hemisphere (wind backs in Southern Hemisphere). This favours the starboard side of the beat. Cold fronts can be recognized by a line of dark clouds, followed by clear skies.

are longer periods of less heavy rain and drizzle. Again the wind veers in the Northern Hemisphere (backs in Southern) but much more slowly (over four to five hours), and it may decrease in strength. Warm fronts are difficult to recognize, but having been warned by the morning's weather map that one is expected, we may distinguish them by a change from clear but cold skies to warmer drizzle. Again the starboard side of the beat is favoured.

3.20

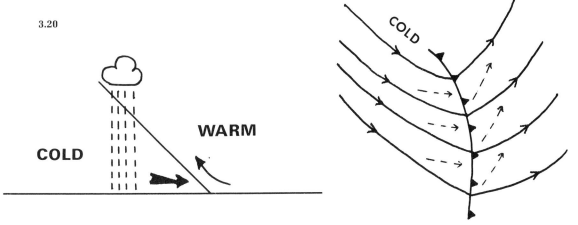

Warm fronts are similar, but more prolonged and gradual (3.21). The arriving warm air slides over the cold air on a more gentle slope and there

3.115 Wind shadows
Behind high banks, woods or clusters of trees, cliffs or large hills there is a 'shadow' where

3.21

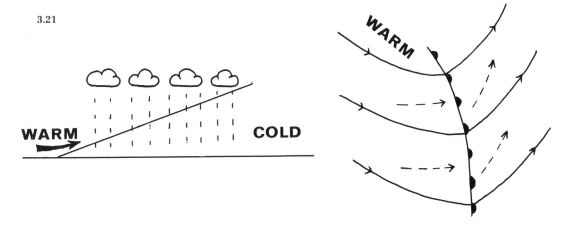

there is less wind than elsewhere. Clearly such areas should be avoided when racing, and it is surprising how far the effect of an obstruction to the wind reaches. The area of reduced wind strength extends downwind to a distance of about twenty times its height (3.22). There may also be a wind bend.

Less clearly appreciated is the fact that such an obstruction also causes a 'shadow' upwind, because the air has to rise to go over it. This effect extends upwind to about ten times the height of the obstruction (3.23).

The length of wind shadow (both types) is reduced if the obstruction is a smooth slope rather than vertical, and for instance wind blowing down off a gentle hill may not reduce in force at all. On water surrounded by cliffs, banks or trees, such as gravel pits or lakes, you should be wary of sailing too far inshore lest you become becalmed while all the others sail past you.

3.12 Tidal Streams and Currents

As we have seen, variations in the wind can make a great difference to the strategy for the

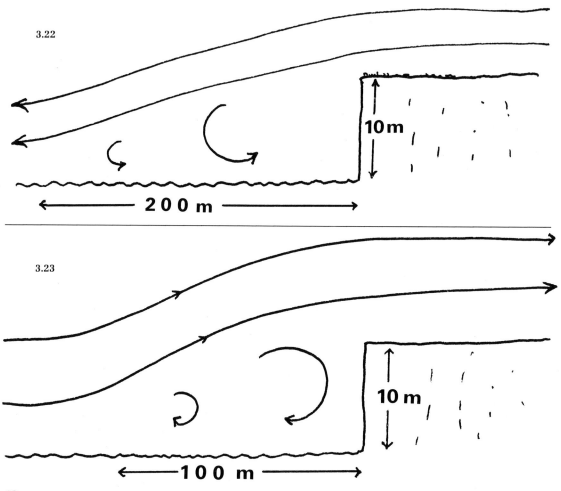

3.22

10 m

200 m

3.23

10 m

100 m

beat, or indeed any other part of the course. Of equal importance is the tidal stream (also sometimes called tidal current), or any other current that may be flowing. There are a number of points to notice about tidal streams.

When sailing boards, it is the horizontal movement of the water that is the aspect of tides that mainly concerns us. This is indeed the result of the vertical rise and fall, and in an enclosed harbour or river estuary one can see the relationship. On open sea, the direction of the tidal stream may not change with the rise and fall, however.

Wherever water has to flow through or past a constriction, it runs faster. This is seen around obstructions, such as the piers of bridges and in narrows and some harbour entrances. It can be very easy to be swept out of a harbour by the strength of this current if you are near the entrance. A similar effect of speeded-up stream occurs off headlands, which act as one-sided bottlenecks.

On the downstream side of harbour break-waters, points of land and sometimes shoals there is an eddy (change of direction and perhaps strength of flow), and during a race these can obviously be used to advantage.

Notice also that the stream runs faster in a deep-water channel than in shallow water near the shore or over sandbanks.

When the tide changes direction there is a period of 'slack' water, but it may be found that the stream changes in the deeper water first while the shallows at the side are still running in the opposite direction or are slack. Often there will be water flowing in opposite directions for a short time.

The basic principle is to get into the stronger stream (deep water) when it is flowing *towards* the next mark, and to find a weaker stream (say, shallow water) or even a different direction of flow (eddies), when it is unfavourable. The direction and strength of the tidal streams, as well as the times at which they will change, can and should all be determined before going afloat.

Often in a race the best strategy for the tide will be the opposite to that for the wind. For instance (3.24a), White goes inshore to get out of unfavourable tide, while Black sails out to sea to benefit from the wind bend. Which one will reach the windward mark first depends on the relative strengths of tide and wind, on the size of the wind bend and on how slack the tide is inshore. In light winds where Black can only just make headway against the tide, White will win. On the other hand, in stronger winds and when the tide is weak anyway Black will win. It is decisions like these that make racing so varied and interesting.

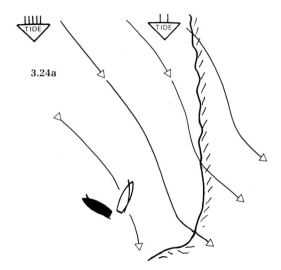

3.24a

3.13 Putting Theory into Practice

Many of the variations in wind and tide discussed above can be determined before even launching the board. Once afloat we sail over as much of the first beating leg as possible before the start, checking on the tide, wind bends, frequency of wind shifts and so on. This period also gives us time to loosen up and to switch our minds to thinking racing.

Before the start, therefore, we should have a good idea of which, if either, side of the course will be favoured. We then have to decide how certain this is. When the favoured side is obvious, have no hesitation in sailing right over to it after the start. Often, however, it is less clear and then we take a more conservative approach, sailing over to the favoured side but without taking an extreme flyer. By doing this we will be in the top tenth of the fleet at the mark if we are right, but if we are wrong we will at least still be *with* the rest of the fleet and not three miles behind them! If neither side is obviously favoured, then we sail up the middle of the beat tacking on wind shifts.

Occasionally the windward mark is not directly upwind of the start, and so more time is spent on one tack than the other. In (3.24b) White sets off on port and Black on starboard. If all remains constant they will both arrive at the mark at the same time. However, if the wind veers when they are halfway up the leg then the situation is that of a wind bend, and White who has sailed towards the centre of the bend comes out in the lead.

Similarly, if the wind bends the other way White will find that she is being lifted up towards the mark while Black, who was already on the lay line, finds that in fact she has

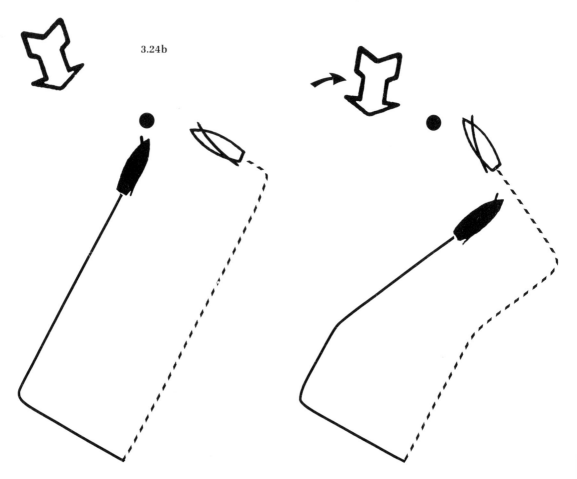

3.24b

overstood the mark. Again White wins. So, unless there are pressing reasons not to, it is preferable to sail on the longer tack first.

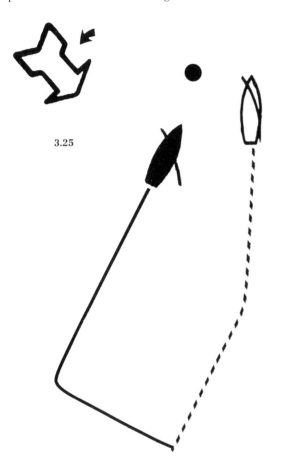

3.25

Once the first beat has been sailed, we are either up with the leaders or in the middle of the fleet. We can then analyse the beat and modify our strategy accordingly so that on the next beat we will be able to sail the optimal course. By the time the last beat comes round, hopefully we will be in the lead with only one or two boards to cover. But if not, then again we modify our strategy and concentrate on improving our position even at this stage of the race.

SUMMARY

SHIFTING WIND
Tack on a backer.
Do not tack on a lift.
A gust means a veer, therefore a lift on starboard tack.

WIND BENDS
Sail the backing tack first – towards the centre of the bend.
If caught on the wrong side of a wind bend cut your losses and tack off.
Watch out for the sea breeze and for frontal systems.

THE TIDE
Stream against you: go into shallower water.
Stream with you: go deeper.

DURING THE RACE
Sail a conservative first beat unless sure your strategy is correct.
If in doubt, sail the longer tack first.

3.2 TACTICS

3.21 Two Boards Meeting on Opposite Tacks

3.211 Starboard tack board well ahead
White has two choices (3.26). She may choose to ignore Black and sail her own course. The initiative is with White: if she holds her course and Black wishes to tack, Black must wait until she is well clear of White's wind shadow.

3.26

Or White may decide to cover Black (3.27). To do this she crosses ahead of Black and then tacks so that she is directly upwind of her. In this position White will maintain her lead even if the wind shifts. The situation is now that of 3.222.

3.27

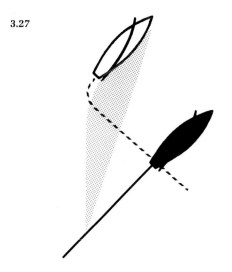

If White's tack does not put Black into dirty wind, Black may decide not to tack.

3.212 Starboard tack board only one length ahead.

Either board may tack off as she wishes until they are close together, when such an action would affect the other. This section deals with boards closer than about four lengths.

White has two choices (3.28): to hold her course or to tack. However, since she is no longer

3.28

3.29

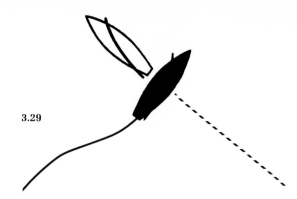

well clear of Black she is unable to tack to cover.

Black has no alternative but to pass under White's stern (3.29). For Black to tack in this position would put her in White's dirty wind (3.30). If Black wants to tack she should wait until she is well clear of White.

3.30

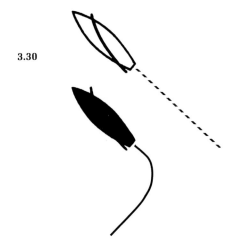

To tack after Black has passed behind her would result in White being lee-bowed by Black. Therefore if White wishes to tack she should do so *before* she crosses ahead of Black. In doing so she gives up her rights of way as starboard tack board and instead, while she is tacking, must keep clear of Black. A collision in this circumstance would result in White's disqualification (Rules 35 and 41). To prevent this White calls out 'Hold your course', so stopping Black from bearing away in anticipation of having to give way to a starboard tack board. Right-of-way is thus transferred to Black who must now maintain a steady course (3.31). White tacks and is now on Black's lee bow (3.32).

3.33

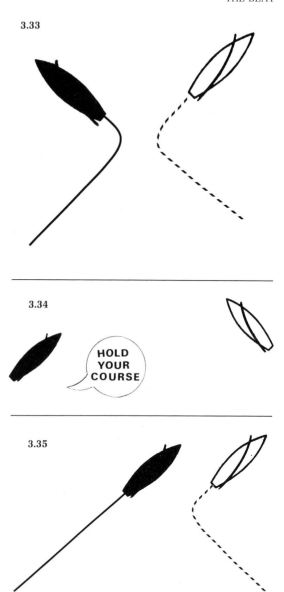

3.31

3.34

3.32

3.35

If Black wants to tack onto starboard then this arrangement is obviously ideal (3.33). However, if Black wishes to stay on port tack she must prevent White from tacking (3.34). To do this she must shout – before White does – 'Hold your course'.

White's only defence to this is to tack immediately (3.35). She should be aware that if she collides with Black she will lose her protest. White is now obliged to maintain her right of way and tacks at considerable risk. Black bears away under White, losing little ground, and continues on port tack.

SUMMARY

If White wishes to continue on starboard, she shouts 'Starboard'. If Black wishes to remain on port she calls 'Hold your course' before White can shout the same.

If White wishes to tack, she shouts 'Hold your course'. If Black wants to tack she either does so well before meeting White, or she hopes that White tacks, or she tacks well after crossing behind White.

3.213 Two boards level

Neither can tack to cover the other, nor can they tack on the other's lee bow. If either wishes to tack she should do so well before meeting the other. Except to avoid a collision, neither board should hail. If White does not shout 'Starboard' Black may hit her and be disqualified. If Black does not shout 'Hold your course' White may attempt to tack (having not seen Black), and will probably hit Black who has borne away to pass beneath her. Black will then protest under Rule 35, Limitations on Altering Course. However, both boards should be aware of Rule 32, Avoiding Collisions Resulting in Serious Damage – although it is unlikely to apply to boards which are both robust and light.

3.214 Starboard tack board one length behind

An interesting position because Black has the initiative despite White's right of way (3.36). However, White may seize the initiative by calling out her intentions. If White does *not* call out Black has two choices: either to tack onto White's lee bow, or to bear away and pass beneath her.

3.36

If Black tacks she should do so sufficiently early so that if she makes a slow tack she is not immediately covered by White (3.37).

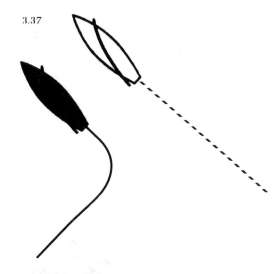

3.37

White must try to sail over Black if possible by freeing off as soon as Black has tacked and taking advantage of her loss of speed in the tack (3.38). Black also sails free and fast until she can lee-bow White (3.39). If this is successful and Black gains a lee-bow position, White tacks off.

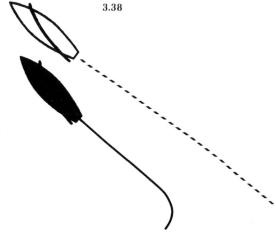

3.38

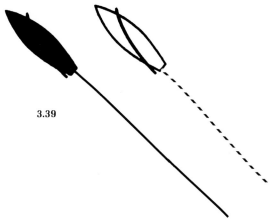

3.39

Alternatively, Black bears away (3.40). This is started as early as possible to minimize loss of speed and distance. White must not attempt to tack to cover Black (3.41), as Black has the advantage of greater speed from bearing away.

3.40

3.41

On the other hand, White may take the initiative by calling her intentions. There are three possibilities:

(i) White stays on starboard: she shouts 'Hold your course' and then passes *beneath* Black. Little distance is lost (3.42), and it avoids the possibility of Black tacking on her lee bow.

3.42

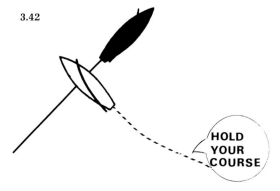

(ii) White tacks. She does this well before meeting Black (3.43) or else she forces the issue by slowing down without altering course, thus preventing Black from passing below her (3.44).

To avoid White, Black tacks since bearing away when this close to White would result in too great a loss of ground, especially in strong winds when bearing away quickly is difficult

3.43

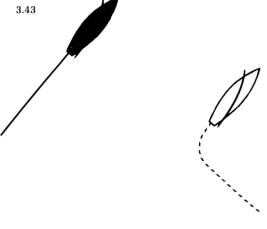

3.44

STARBOARD!

(see 3.37). White can then tack off into clear wind.

(iii) White tries to persuade Black to tack too early, so giving White a good covering position with the possibility of winning their next encounter. To do this White shouts 'Starboard!' as loudly and fiercely as possible, suggesting to Black that if she does not tack immediately, if not sooner, she will ram White. (Black then panics, and tacks.)

Black's defence is of course to know that White is where she is, and so not to be fooled by such a frantic call. Black responds with 'Hold your course!' and then decides whether or not to tack in her own time.

If this does not work White resorts to one of the previous tactics. *Great care* must be taken in using tactic (i) now, since having claimed right of way in (iii) it would be extremely difficult to prove in a protest that it was then relinquished to Black as in (i).

3.215 Port board well ahead

The tactics are identical to those of 3.211, substituting Black for White and *vice versa* throughout.

3.22 Two Boards on the Same Tack

3.221 White clear ahead

White must decide whether to sail her own course or to cover Black. This depends on her overall position in the fleet, and also on the importance of beating Black. If White is leading the race she will decide to cover Black, but if White is tenth and it's only the first or second beat, or even the last beat of one of the early races

in the series, then White will choose to ignore Black and try to improve her overall position without getting slowed down in a battle with Black.

Unless Black is more than about three lengths behind White, she is in White's dirty wind and is in great danger of dropping off to leeward into an even worse position, so she tacks off (3.45).

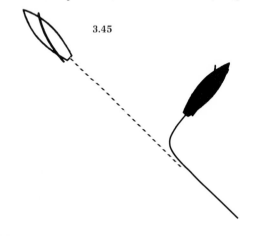

3.45

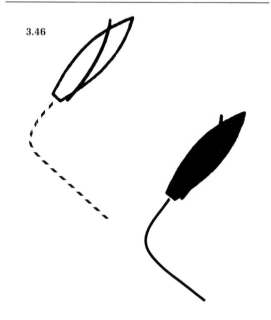

3.46

If White decides to cover Black she should tack as soon as Black does (3.46). The position is now that of 3.223.

3.222 White ahead and to windward

In this position White will maintain her lead even if the wind shifts, regardless of whether it heads or lifts her (3.47). This is therefore the ideal position for White to be in to cover Black. Again, White must consider whether or not to cover Black in the light of her overall position in the race and the series.

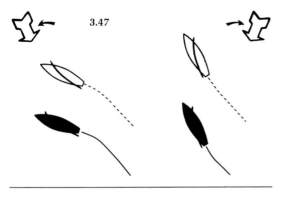

3.47

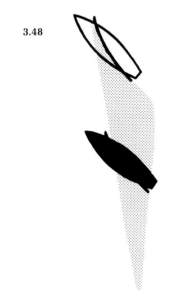

3.48

White decides to cover Black and so tries to keep her in her dirty wind (3.48). Unless she is in clear wind and there are pressing reasons for staying on this tack, Black tacks off to try to break White's cover (3.49).

3.49

If Black tacks, White may ignore her or may also tack to cover (3.50). Black is again effectively covered and so she tacks off once again.

A tacking match has developed and these manoeuvres may be repeated many times. As soon as possible White must decide which of them is tacking faster. If White is quicker she should encourage the tacking match by making sure she always tacks directly onto Black's wind. She will then gradually draw farther ahead with each tack (3.51).

Tacking matches slow both boards down considerably. Black must consider whether she can afford to concentrate on White or whether she should break away to race against the rest of the fleet. Black also decides if she is tacking

3.50

3.51

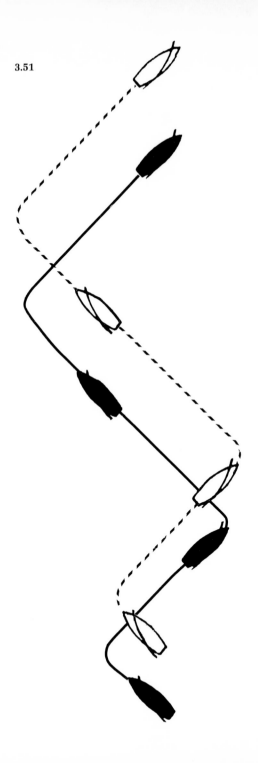

faster or slower than White. If faster, and she can afford to continue the match against White, she should do so. If she cannot afford to waste time on a tacking match, or if White is tacking better, Black must break cover as soon as possible.

Breaking Cover (see also 3.234)

Black starts by analysing the sequence of moves: does White start her tack as soon as Black starts hers, or does she wait until Black has finished her turn? Does she watch Black, or does she just listen for the crack of Black's sails to tell her that Black has tacked?

(i) *White starts tack before Black has finished hers.* Black breaks cover by doing a dummy tack (3.52): she starts to turn normally, but making plenty of noise about it so that White gets ready to tack herself. As soon as White starts her tack Black bears away back onto her original course

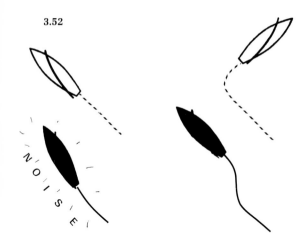

3.52

and the two boards sail off on opposite tacks. White cannot tack back again quick enough to cover Black, and if she tried she would lose so much speed that Black would come out in the lead.

(ii) White starts tack after Black has finished hers. Black puts in a very quiet but fast tack so that White notices as late as possible (3.53). As soon as White starts her tack Black tacks back again.

Once her cover has been broken White concentrates on sailing her own course as fast as possible until the two boards meet again.

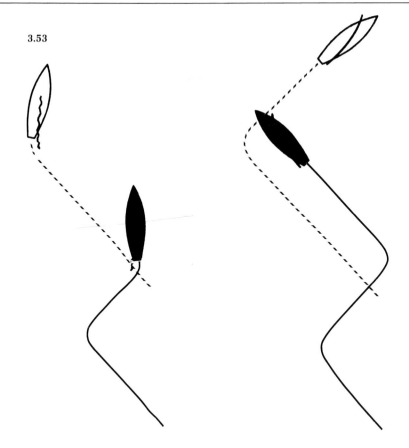

3.53

(iii) White tacks when she hears the crack of Black's sail. Black eases out her sail and then pumps violently to make it crack as loudly as possible – without tacking (3.54). White hears the noise, thinks that Black has tacked, and so tacks off to cover leaving Black in peace!

3.54

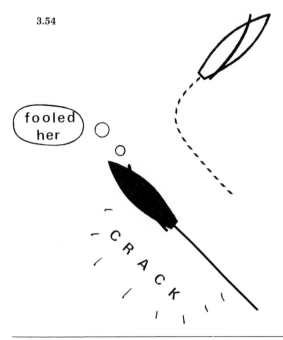

3.223 White abeam to windward

White may choose either to cover Black or to sail her own course.

(i) White covers. She sails free and fast over Black (3.55) until she is on Black's wind, taking care not to infringe Rule 37.1 – Windward Board Keeps Clear.

Black may prevent this by herself freeing off (3.56). However, this results in both losing ground to the rest of the fleet, and so should only be used when well ahead or if the other competitors need not be considered with regard to the series standings.

White will be able to prevent Black from tacking off by coming close enough to her (about half a length).

Black may tack off, but this has to be done early since White will be able to prevent her from tacking if Black allows her to come too close.

Black having tacked, White again has the choice of ignoring her or of tacking immediately to cover, hoping to achieve the position of 3.222.

(ii) White does not cover. Black may either sail as fast as possible, ignoring White, or she may try to sail high to lee-bow White (3.57). If this is achieved White is forced to tack off.

3.55

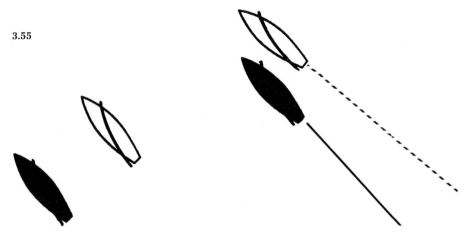

3.56

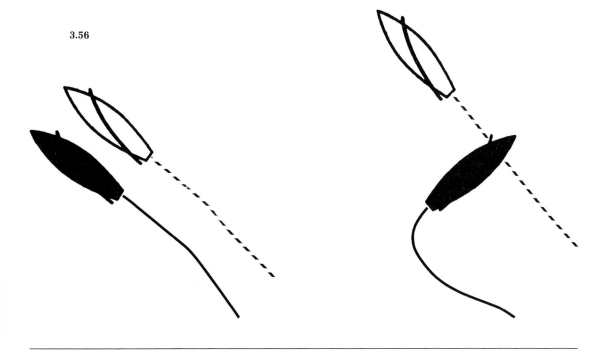

3.57

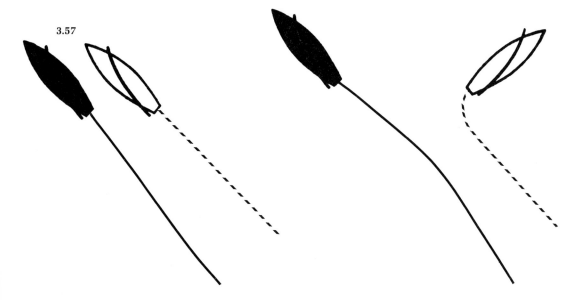

However this is a risky tactic, since if Black fails to reach the lee-bow position she will be left in White's dirty wind with no room to tack out of it (3.58).

Finally, Black may tack off behind White (right, 3.58).

Again, White has the choice of tacking to cover (position as in 3.222).

3.224 White on Black's windward quarter

White is being lee-bowed by Black (3.59). Unless there are good reasons not to (see 4.21), White tacks off immediately.

Black does not follow her tack since to do so would put her in the same position that White was in.

3.58

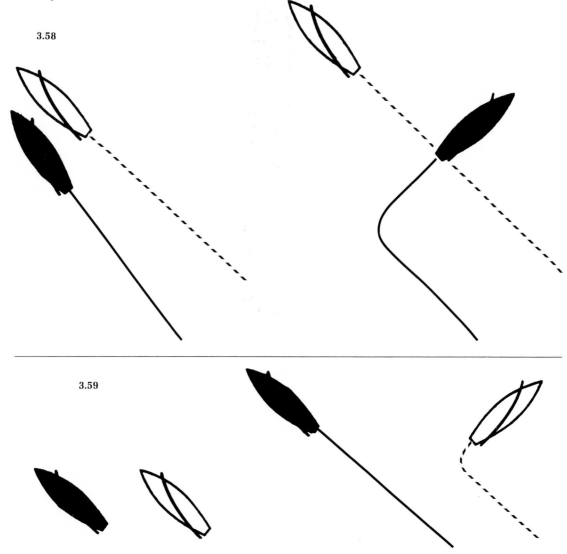

3.59

3.23 Three Boards Meeting on Opposite Tacks

3.231 White leads – Covering two opponents

In this situation it is easy for White to cover either Grey or Black, as in the previous section (3.222). However, in doing so she stands the risk of losing her lead to the board she doesn't cover. To avoid this White covers both boards together. This can only be done by 'herding' Black and Grey so that both are always on the same tack. Grey, the third board, is the one that decides the tack. White then persuades Black to choose the same tack as Grey by covering her closely until she tacks, as follows:

White tacks onto Black's wind, leaving her room so that she can tack off (3.60). Black then tacks out of White's dirty wind (3.61).

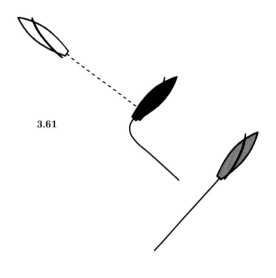

3.61

3.60

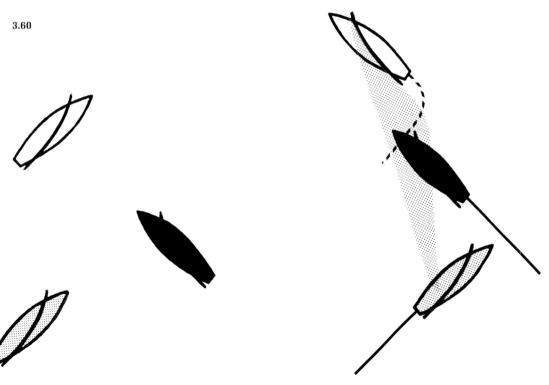

Black and Grey are now on the same tack so White also tacks to cover both of them *loosely*, taking care *not* to take Black's wind (3.62). If Black feels that she is in dirty wind she will tack off so breaking White's double cover.

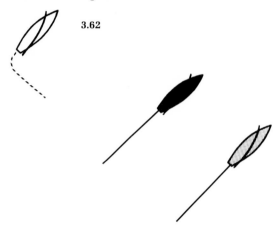

3.62

If this happens White must induce Black to tack back again. She does this by herself tacking to cover Black *closely* (3.63). Black is again persuaded to tack off.

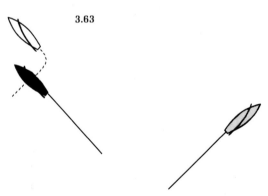

3.63

Thus, when Black is on the correct tack (from White's point of view) she is covered only loosely (3.64), but if she goes onto the 'wrong' tack she is covered tightly until she tacks back again.

When Grey decides to tack, then Black must be induced to tack as well. White sails down to

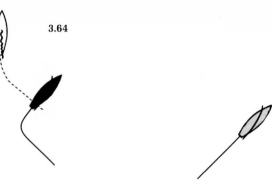

3.64

cover Black tightly (3.65) until she follows Grey onto the new tack (3.66).

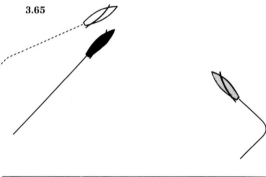

3.65

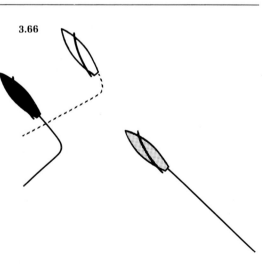

3.66

In this way White can loosely cover two opponents. However, it can be seen that it involves White slowing down at times in order to cover Black tightly. Therefore this tactic will normally be reserved for the end of the last beat. It is important that White does not get into a tacking match with Black, since this will quickly result in Grey sailing through into the lead.

3.232 White is second of three boards

A difficult position (3.67). Tactics will depend on White's position in the series as a whole; she must consider whether to keep her position as second – covering Grey with the tactics described in Section 3.21 – or whether to ignore Grey and go for first place. In the latter case White must concentrate on breaking Black's cover so that she can sail her own course instead of being herded. Again the tactics of Section 3.21 apply, but White must be aware of the risk of letting Grey through to the lead leaving Black and White to fight for second and third.

3.67

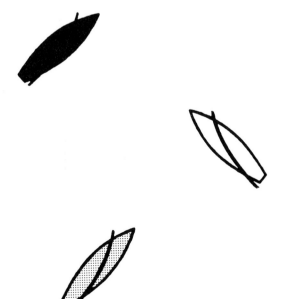

3.233 White is third

White may find she is being ignored as Black and Grey fight their own private battle, in which case she sails off on her own course, often straight into the lead (3.68). However, if Black is herding, White should start her own tacking match. One of three things will happen:

3.68

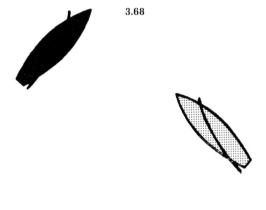

(*i*) She will be ignored, in which case she is free of cover.
(*ii*) Grey will cover her while Black sails off in the lead. Tactics of 3.21 apply.
(*iii*) Black attempts to cover both Grey and White. This last possibility occurs frequently in team racing, and is the one we will consider here.

Every time White tacks, Black tries to force Grey to follow suit. This requires Black to be sufficiently close that she can cover Grey tightly. Both Black and Grey are thus slowed down more than White during the tacking match. Eventually either Grey will break Black's cover and White will suddenly find herself free, or the situation below will occur.

3.69

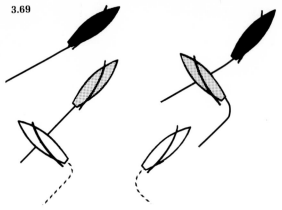

White tacks (3.69). Black tightens her cover on Grey who then tacks also. As Grey is tacking, White tacks back.

Black then tacks onto Grey to force her to tack back (3.70). As Grey again tacks, White also tacks. She will find that she is now in a position to call on Grey.

Grey will have to tack because of the close proximity of the boards (3.71). Without rushing, White tacks back again. White is now free. If she tacks shortly to rejoin the fray she will find that when they next meet she will certainly be second, and may well be able to challenge Black.

3.71

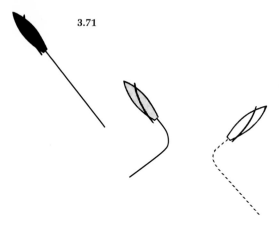

3.70

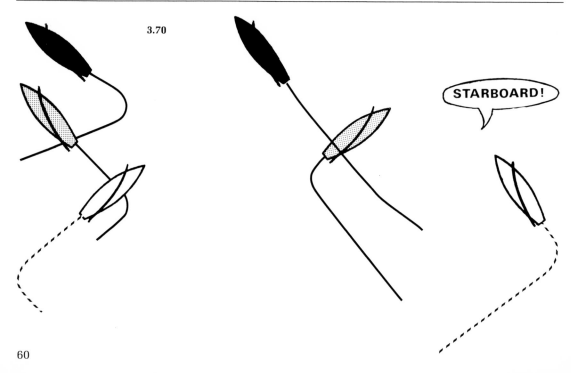

STARBOARD!

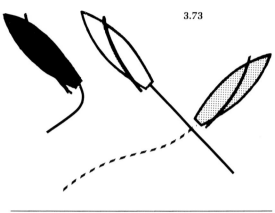

3.234 Black covers White on port tack, Grey on starboard

White's tactics   White uses this situation to break Black's cover. White passes behind Grey (3.72). Black then tacks to give way to Grey, and White sails free (3.73).

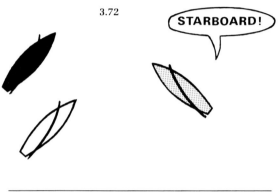

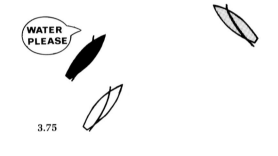

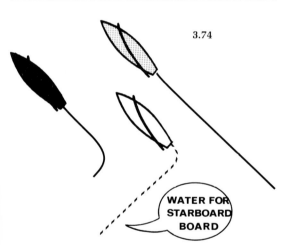
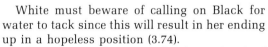

White must beware of calling on Black for water to tack since this will result in her ending up in a hopeless position (3.74).

Black's tactics   If Grey is level or ahead of Black, Black calls on White for water to pass behind Grey (3.75). Black bears away, and by virtue of her increase in speed will sail over White, so maintaining her cover (3.76).

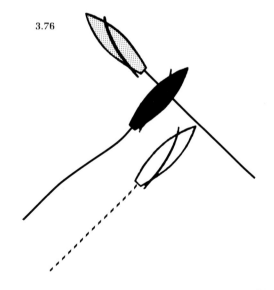

3.77

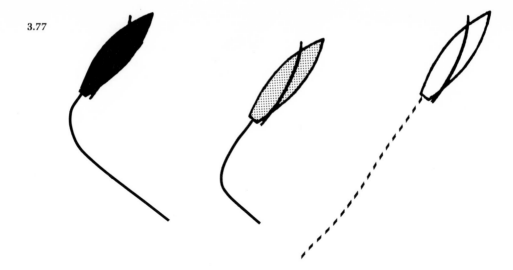

If Grey is behind Black (as in 3.72), then Black tacks and attempts to lee-bow Grey. Grey is forced to tack (3.77), and after a short while Black can tack back onto port so covering White indirectly.

White is now in clear air, and may stay on port as long as she likes. Alternatively (3.78), she may tack (without getting in Grey's water) and come in on starboard. White then deals with Grey and Black separately, using the tactics for two boards (Section 3.21).

3.78

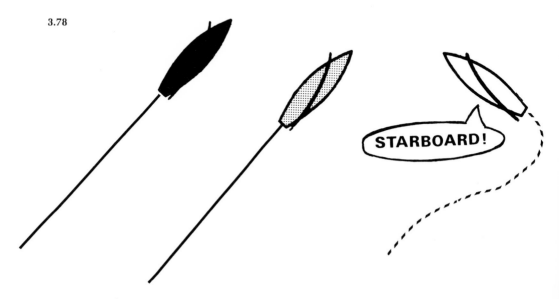

STARBOARD!

It is worth reflecting that if White can force Grey to tack (3.79) she may find herself in a commanding position particularly useful near a mark (see Chapter 4).

3.24 Three Boards on the Same Tack

3.241 White to windward
Whatever the exact relative positions of three boards, White may either ignore the two to leeward or she may cover one or both of them, in which case the tactics are those of Sections 3.22 and 3.231 respectively.

3.242 White in the middle
On the whole, tactics are those of Section 3.22 (two boards on same tack) and are directed against Black or Grey as circumstances dictate. However, there is one position worthy of mention simply because it is to be avoided at all costs: that shown in (3.80). A drastic position. White is lee-bowed by Grey and prevented from tacking by Black with the result that she is gradually squeezed out by the other two, ending up in Black's dirty wind. If White ever gets into this position she must quickly slow herself down so that she can tack out, crossing behind Grey.

This tactic is fequently used in team racing.

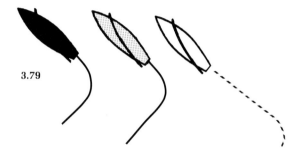

3.79

For example, Grey and Black are on the opposite team to White. By preventing White from tacking they can slow her down from second to last place, letting their team-mate through ahead of them. The secret is for Black to slow down with White, making sure that she cannot tack away; often slowing down to the point where both are standing still with their sails flapping! This position is impossible for White to escape from if it is well applied by the other team.

3.243 White to leeward
White's tactics will be directed to getting clear air and breaking cover. She will use the tactics of Sections 3.22, 3.231 and 3.234, and also the tactics of Grey in the special position described immediately above.

3.80

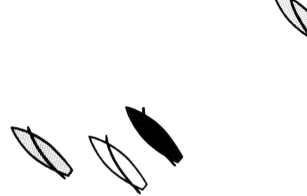

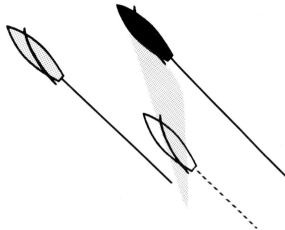

4
The Windward Mark

The approach to the windward mark is as crucial as its actual rounding, and if both are handled correctly many places may be gained.

4.1 ROUNDING IN A LARGE FLEET

4.11 Mark Left to Port

This is the most common situation, and in setting a course is much to be preferred to a starboard hand course. Since the mark is to be left to port, boards must be on starboard tack to go round it. This results in a whole line on starboard, queueing to round.

In (4.1), which shows this situation, all the **White boards** have right of way over the Black boards.

A is on the lay line and will easily round the mark.

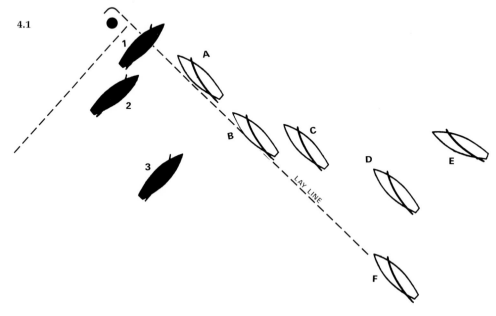

4.1

B is on the lay line, but because she is in A's dirty wind she will drop down to leeward and will not be able to lay the mark. Because of this she will have to go right round and rejoin the queue, probably in last place.

C To allow for this drift to leeward, C deliberately overstood the mark and so will lay it comfortably.

D also overstood to allow for leeward drift and will also lay the mark. Notice that she has overstood even farther than C to make sure that she will make the mark, unlike B.

E has overstood too much: she will actually have to bear away for the mark and so has lost valuable ground.

F Although above the lay line, F is in dirty wind and so will not lay the mark. She realizes this and tacks off to join the queue.

Of the **Black boards**:

1 may be able to sail between A and the mark (remember that A has right of way and will probably call). She then tacks to windward of A, and rounds the mark on A's windward quarter (4.2).

2 tries to round by tacking under A (4.3). As soon as she has finished her tack she is entitled to water to round the mark (Rule 42.3 a (ii)). However, if she fails to lay the mark she is in a hopeless situation and will have to join the queue.

4.2

4.3

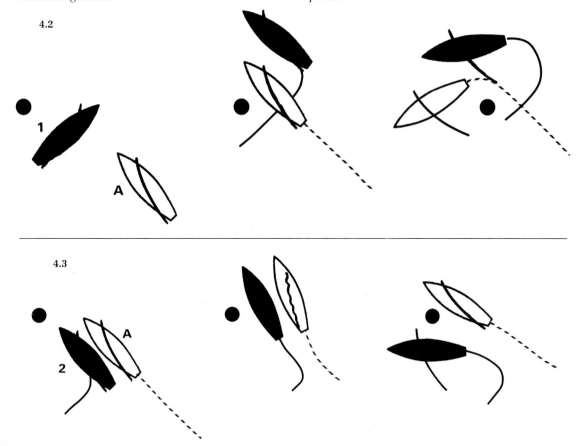

3 is probably in a better position than 1 or 2 since she has room to look for a gap through which she can go (4.4). She sees such a gap between C and D, and so sails behind B and C and tacks onto D's lee bow. Once there she sails high to keep clear of C's lee bow, and to prevent D from sailing over her. She comfortably lays the mark.

When coming up to a windward mark with a number of boards, the best approach is that of 3. By joining the lay line too early boards D and E have had to overstand considerably, thus increasing the distance they have to sail. 3 avoids this problem by joining the lay line later, when she can determine exactly where it is, and yet not

4.4

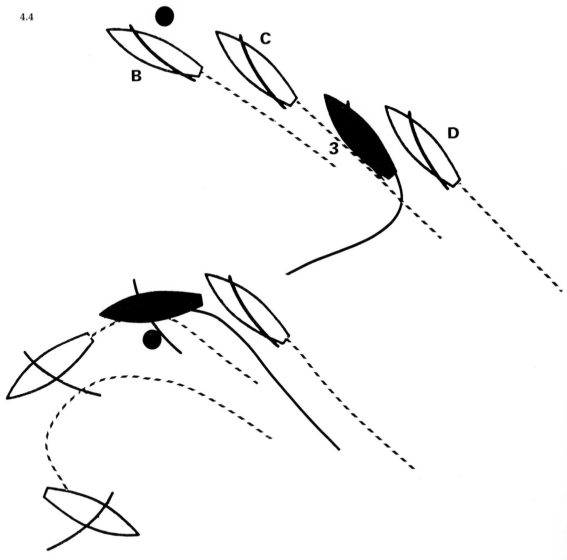

so close (like 1 and 2) that she is unable to find a gap in which to join the queue. The approaches of 1 and 2 may be highly effective if they come off, but are exceedingly risky and not normally to be recommended.

4.12 Mark Left to Starboard

The problem with starboard-hand courses is clearly shown by the situation in (4.5).

1 is the first to the mark. However, she is on port tack and will not be able to clear A who is on starboard. So she has to tack off, letting A through to the lead. B is immediately behind A and so prevents her from tacking for the mark (4.6). This places B in the lead.

However, C saw what B did and tries it herself. B has no intention of letting C through to the lead, and so she luffs head-to-wind (4.7). She tells

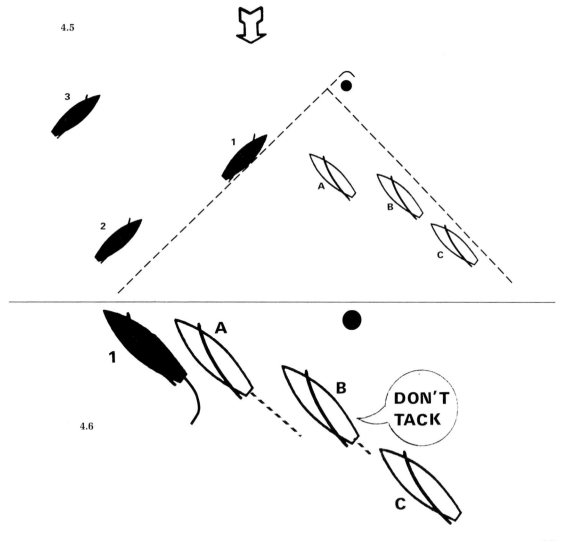

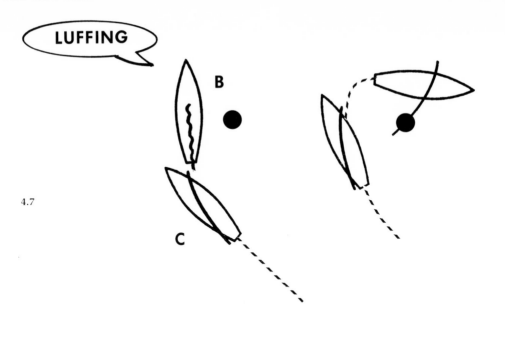

4.7

C what she is doing so that C does not accuse her of tacking in her water. As soon as C is overlapped to leeward, B can tack and round the mark.

The overall position is now as shown in (4.8). B is now in the lead, and 1, who had been first to the mark, has been pushed back to fourth or fifth simply because she came in on port tack. B has clearly handled the situation best, but now let us consider C.

C is on starboard and in position to tack around the mark following B, but 2 can prevent her from tacking in her water (Rule 41.1) and tells her so. C then has to sail on a starboard tack and let 2 round first.

However, C defends her position by spilling wind and slowing down without altering her course (4.9). 2 is then forced to either tack or bear away (in which case she would not lay the mark). C is then free to tack for the mark.

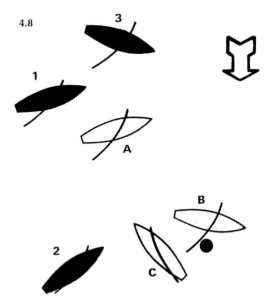

4.8

4.9

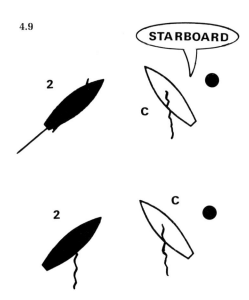

STARBOARD

2 counters this by herself slowing down so that she can pass behind C without having to bear away, and so she can still lay the mark to round ahead if C moves.

This situation may end up with both boards standing still and waiting for the other to move first. Unless there are other competitors to consider, each should try to out-wait the other. Whoever moves first will let the other round the mark first. For the sake of argument we will assume that C won this particular clash. The order round the mark is then as in (4.10).

The ideal approach for a starboard-hand windward mark is therefore on starboard tack, making sure that there is room in which to tack for the mark either by luffing sharply (when there is a board immediately astern) or by slowing down to force a port-tack opponent to tack off. These two methods are demonstrated by B and C above.

4.10

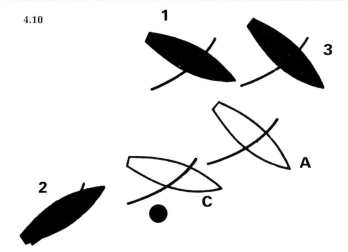

4.2 ROUNDING WITH ONE OPPONENT

4.21 The Approach to the Mark

In this section the tactics are the same whether the windward mark is to be left to port or to starboard. Provided neither board is actually clear ahead of the other, they are both in a position to reach the mark first (4.11). The principle to follow is to keep between the mark and your opponent. We will first consider the ideal situation (in which the opponent does not defend herself), which is in fact all too common. We will then discuss a more complex situation in which both boards fully understand the tactics involved.

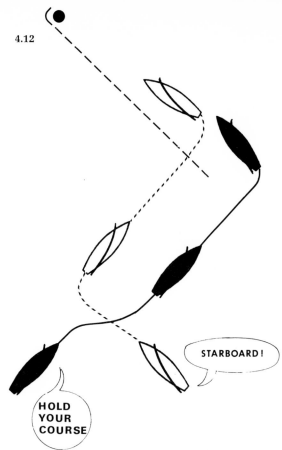

4.12

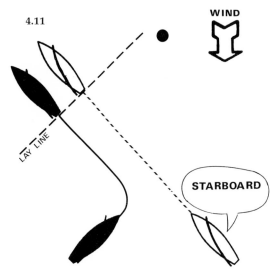

4.11

4.211 Ideal situation, White on starboard

(i) White calls 'Starboard' and Black tacks (4.11). White then sails on, preventing Black from tacking, until well past the lay line. White then tacks for the mark and Black follows. White rounds in the lead.

(ii) White calls 'Starboard' and Black bears away (4.12). As Black passes behind her White tacks onto her windward quarter. White should be

sufficiently close that Black does not have room to tack, but should be far enough away so as to be clear of Black's lee-bow. Often a lee-bow situation will be unavoidable, but as long as White is in a position to stop Black from tacking it matters little if she is slowed down slightly by a lee-bow. However, if this is attempted too far from the mark Black may be able to escape and tack ahead of White.

White sails Black past the lay line before tacking.

4.212 Ideal situation, White on port

Black calls 'Starboard'. White does not tack but passes behind her (4.13). As soon as she has passed behind Black, White tacks.

4.13

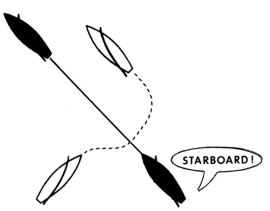

White can now stop Black from tacking for the mark, and so sails her past the lay line (4.14). White tacks when she can easily make the mark and rounds ahead of Black.

4.14

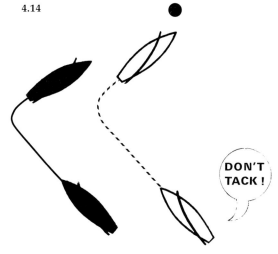

4.213 Complex situation
Both boards are the same distance from the mark. White calls 'Starboard'. Black is not confident she can clear White's bow and so she

bears away and crosses behind her (4.15). As soon as Black passes behind her White tacks, but she must beware of Black tacking simultaneously as Black will have right of way.

4.15

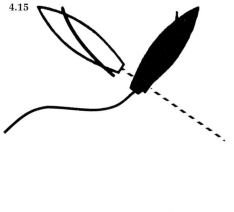

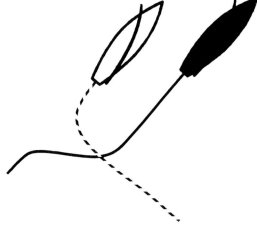

As soon as she clears White, Black tacks (4.16). She has right of way over White should she also tack, under Rule 41.4 – Simultaneous Taking or Gybing. White is now prevented from tacking and so returns to starboard tack. However, she has gained some distance upwind and she should now be able to lee-bow Black.

White cannot tack for the mark so she luffs Black as much as possible and as sharply as possible, without warning (4.17). If White luffs

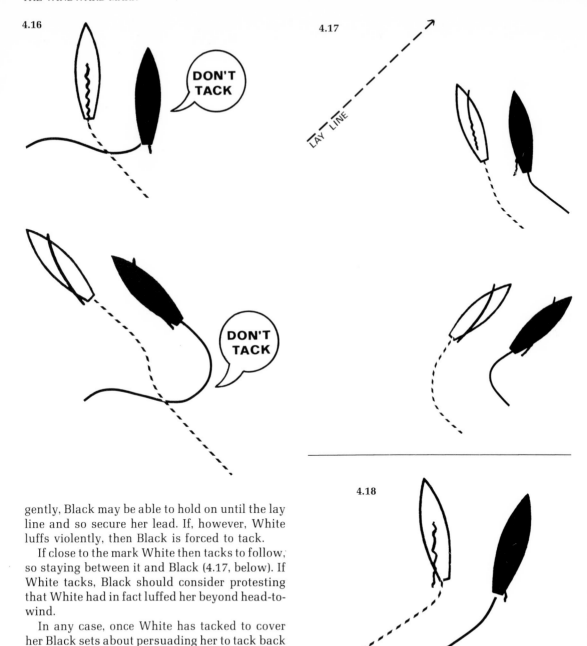

gently, Black may be able to hold on until the lay line and so secure her lead. If, however, White luffs violently, then Black is forced to tack.

If close to the mark White then tacks to follow, so staying between it and Black (4.17, below). If White tacks, Black should consider protesting that White had in fact luffed her beyond head-to-wind.

In any case, once White has tacked to cover her Black sets about persuading her to tack back again. Black luffs violently (4.18). White having tacked off, Black then tacks in her own time

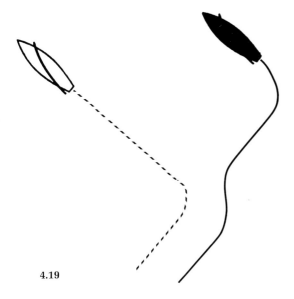

4.19

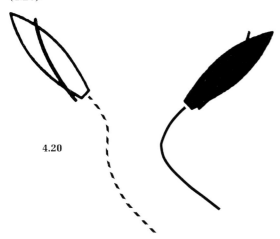

4.20

If White does not tack in the first place, then Black regains her speed and tacks as soon as possible in her own time. Again she can control White (4.21).

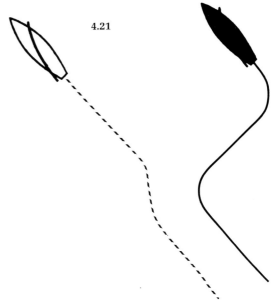

4.21

(4.19). She is tacking onto starboard and so can control White from a greater distance than if they were both on port.

If the windward mark is still far away, then after luffing Black (see 4.17), White does not tack since Black would then have plenty of time in which to escape. Instead, White sails her own course to the next mark until they meet again (4.20).

4.22 Close to the Mark: Mark Left to Port

As they approach the mark, either one board will be successfully covering the other or the battle will still be on. In the latter case both should concentrate on getting to the starboard lay line first, making sure they do not overstand the mark. In this case White has reached the lay line first (4.22).

Black cannot lay the mark if she tacks beneath White and so must pass behind her. If White then fails to lay the mark, Black will be coming in on starboard and White will be stuck. However, if White overstands the mark, Black will tack below her (4.23).

Should the boards meet (Black is on starboard) before reaching the lay line, but close to the mark (4.24), White decides to give way, since she will then be able to reach the starboard lay

73

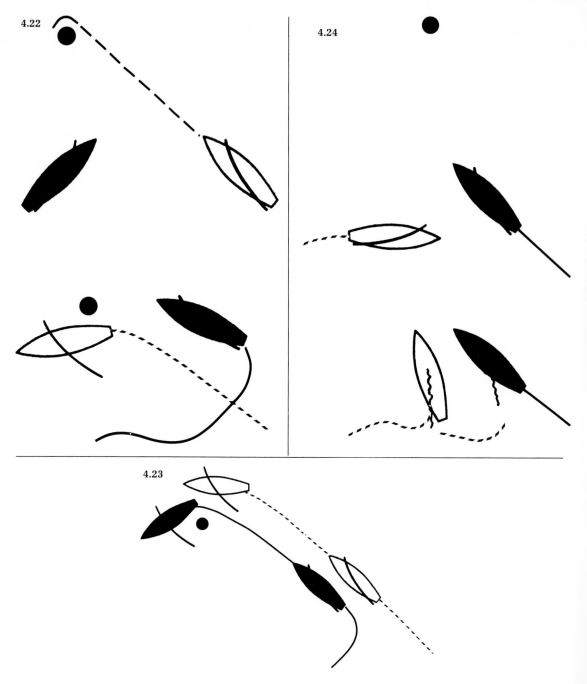

4.22

4.24

4.23

line first. To counter this, Black slows down without altering course.

White is then forced to tack to avoid her and so Black tacks as well, reaching the starboard-tack lay line first (4.25). White can defend herself by also slowing down, so that she can still pass behind Black (see 4.24).

Whoever reaches the starboard lay line accurately and first will round the mark first.

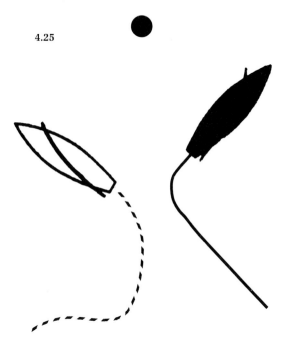

4.25

4.231 White under-stands the mark

Black bears away for White and then tacks onto the lay line (4.26). Black can then prevent White from tacking for the mark, and will round first (4.27).

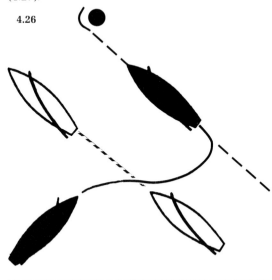

4.26

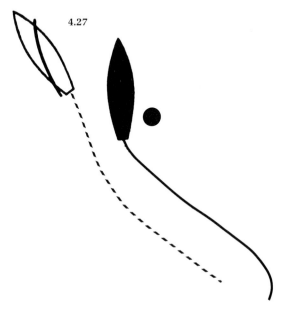

4.27

4.23 Close to the Mark: Mark Left to Starboard

The tactics for the approach to the mark have been discussed in Section 4.21. If neither board is in a commanding position, both should concentrate on being the first to the starboard lay line, as in 4.22 above. For a mark to be left to starboard it matters little if the lay line is overstood, indeed it is preferable to over-stand slightly rather than under-stand.

75

White avoids this by herself tacking as soon as Black passes below her (4.28). She then sails Black past the lay line and tacks for the mark in her own time.

4.28

Black's defence to this is to tack as soon as she sees that White is tacking (4.29). As they are then tacking simultaneously, White must keep clear (Rule 41.4).

4.232 White on the lay line, Black one length ahead

Black tacks on White's lee bow (4.30), and then luffs violently until White ducks to leeward of her — or even tacks off! (4.31). Black can then reassume her course knowing she will be first to the mark (4.33).

4.30

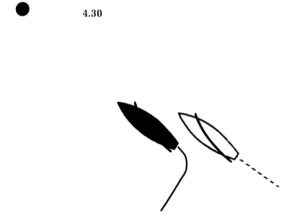

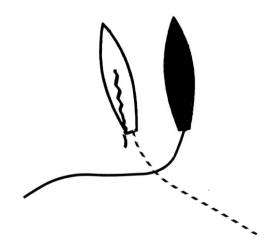

4.29

There is little that White can do about this, so she takes care not to overlap Black to leeward while staying as close to her stern as possible, preferably with a slight overlap to windward, in the hope of preventing Black from tacking to round the mark (4.32).

Black counters this by luffing hard at the mark until White passes her to leeward (4.34) and Black can then tack round.

4.233 White on the lay line, Black level or behind

Black passes behind White and then tacks onto her windward quarter, trying to stop White from tacking at the mark (4.35).

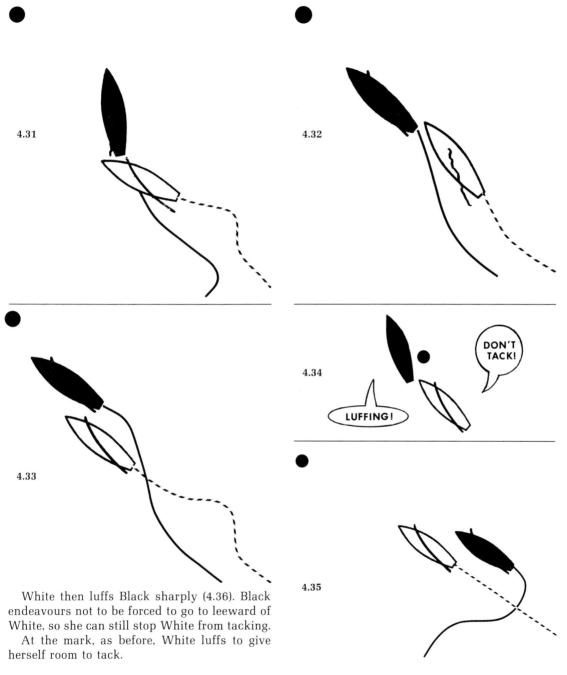

4.31

4.32

4.33

4.34

LUFFING!

DON'T TACK!

4.35

White then luffs Black sharply (4.36). Black endeavours not to be forced to go to leeward of White, so she can still stop White from tacking.

At the mark, as before, White luffs to give herself room to tack.

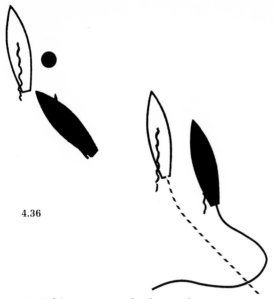

4.36

4.234 White over-stands the mark

A safe position for White (4.37). Black can do little unless she is prepared to go to great lengths just to beat her. Black should not consider any sort of attack unless there are no other opponents to consider, for instance if Black and White are miles ahead of the rest of the fleet or in the last race of a series when Black only has to finish ahead of White to win the series.

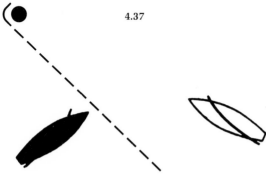

4.37

If there are other opponents to consider

Black should be content with following White

round the mark. If Black is slightly ahead she tacks onto White's lee-bow (4.38). Once within two lengths of the mark, White is entitled to water for the mark and rounds first. However, if Black establishes her lee-bow early enough, she

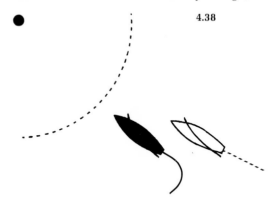

4.38

may be able to pull far enough ahead to break White's overlap before the two length limit.

If Black cannot make a lee-bow, she should tack onto White's windward quarter (4.39). She is unlikely to be able to stop White from

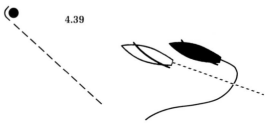

4.39

rounding the mark, but she will lose less ground than if she tacks below her.

When White is the only opponent

In this case Black goes all out to beat White and can afford to use tactics that will slow both boards down considerably. Black tacks underneath White (4.38) so that she can luff her past the mark (see Rule 42.1 d – Room at Marks when Overlapped). If Black is ahead of White she then luffs sharply and as high as possible without

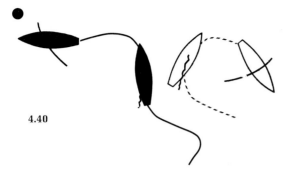

4.40

loosing her luffing rights, to force White to tack (4.40).

If Black is level with White any luff at all would allow White to call 'Mast abeam' and so foil Black's plans. Instead Black merely carries on closehauled (4.41). Since they have both

overstood the mark this is equivalent to a luff. If White does not tack away, Black continues to sail her the wrong side of the mark until well past it, when she can bear away, gybing if necessary, to round the mark correctly and ahead of White.

4.3 ROUNDING ALONE

The correct way to round any mark is that which requires the least change of direction.

RIGHT: White chooses the lay line so that she only has to bear away to round the mark. The change in direction is about 90° and a good speed is kept up through the turn.

WRONG: Because she has to tack around the mark, Black has to turn through about 180° in order to go off onto the same heading and is slowed down considerably.

4.41

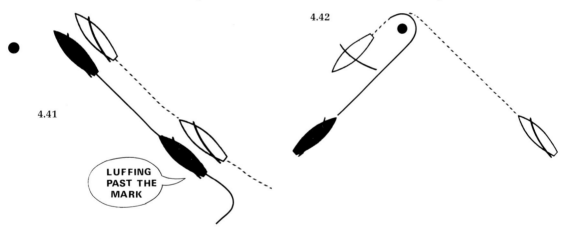

LUFFING
PAST THE
MARK

4.42

5
The First Reach

The tactics for this leg are the same for both port and starboard hand courses.

5.1 SAILING ALONE—OVERALL STRATEGY

When sailing this reach it is important to know what would be the fastest course if there were no other competitors in the way. This ideal route is what is called the 'Proper Course' in the Definitions section of the Racing Rules and is the term we shall use here. However, the proper course is not necessarily a straight line from the windward mark to the gybe mark, as we shall soon see.

5.11 Effects of Tide

In the absence of any tidal stream the proper course is indeed a straight line from one mark to the other. However if there is a tide or current running it must be taken into account. If the stream is flowing upwind, then if White simply aimed straight for the next buoy after rounding the windward mark she would end up sailing a large arc as she was constantly swept upwind of the rhumb line (5.1).

To avoid this, as soon as White rounds the windward mark she lines up the wing mark with a fixed object such as a building or tree on the shore (5.2). She then bears away and sails so that these two points remain in line. By doing this she

5.1

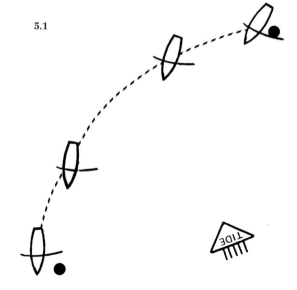

aims lower than the mark and ends up actually sailing a straight line over the ground (5.3).

If the stream flows downwind (5.4) White must be especially careful not to drop below the rhumb line, since she will then have to harden up to lay the mark, thus losing speed (never mind the greater distance), and she may even find that she cannot lay the mark without tacking. This problem occurs particularly often when the reach is very close, or becomes close because of a

5.2

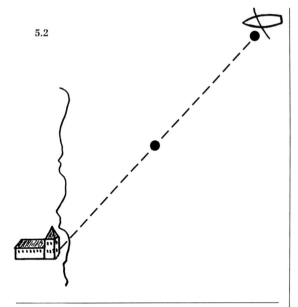

5.3

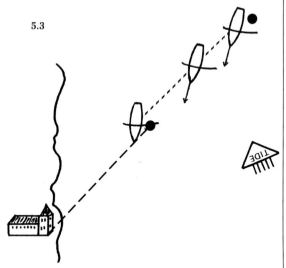

5.4

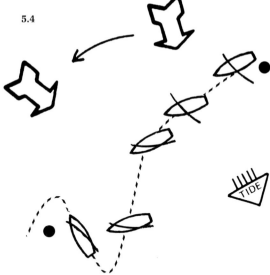

For this reason, if the tide is flowing downwind White starts the leg by sailing very high (5.5). She then estimates the strength of the tide as it rushes past the windward mark and checks whether the leg is a close fetch or a broad reach. If the tide is very strong and/or the course is a close fetch, White decides to continue sailing very high, keeping an eye on a shore-based transit with the idea of staying well above the

5.5

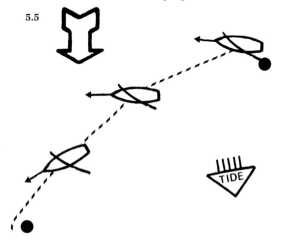

wind shift. In (5.4) Black had lined up a transit with the wing mark and was sailing a fast straight course to the mark. However the wind then backed 30°–40° and now she cannot lay the mark even though she is now sailing close-hauled.

rhumb line. It is easier to have to bear away for the mark if one has sailed too high than to have to tack for it after ending up too low. When she is sure she will be able to lay the mark, White may decide to sail a slightly lower course.

On this leg it is useful to watch whether any boards ahead are having difficulty laying the mark. Here White sees that Black has had to tack up for the mark, and so she stays closehauled until she is sure she can lay the mark herself even if the wind should shift again (5.6).

5.12 Using the Wind and Waves

Sailboards are lightweight craft that accelerate fast. It is therefore important to exploit the variations in wind and waves as much as possible to obtain the maximum speed from the board. Whenever possible, you should ride the waves and plane off in the gusts irrespective of direction.

Here White catches the waves in the gusts and rides them as long as possible (5.7). When the gust ends she then points slightly higher to get back on course, and compensates for being set downwind by the wave, until the next gust arrives. In this way she actually sails a rather wiggly line, but does so at top speed and so easily overtakes those who hold a straight course.

5.2 SAILING WITH ONE OPPONENT

5.21 Overtaking

5.211 Overtaking to leeward

White is a fair distance behind Black but is obviously a threat, and so Black will be looking back frequently to see whether or not she is

5.6

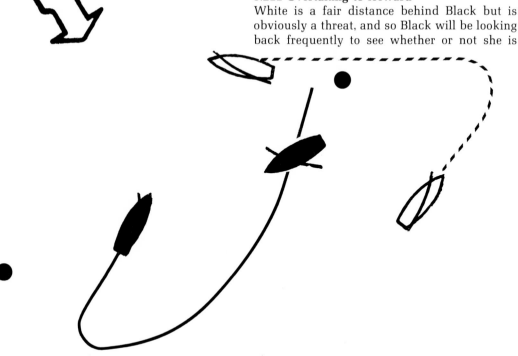

gaining. This in itself often ruins Black's concentration and confidence. White turns this to even greater advantage by encouraging Black to over-react in defending herself.

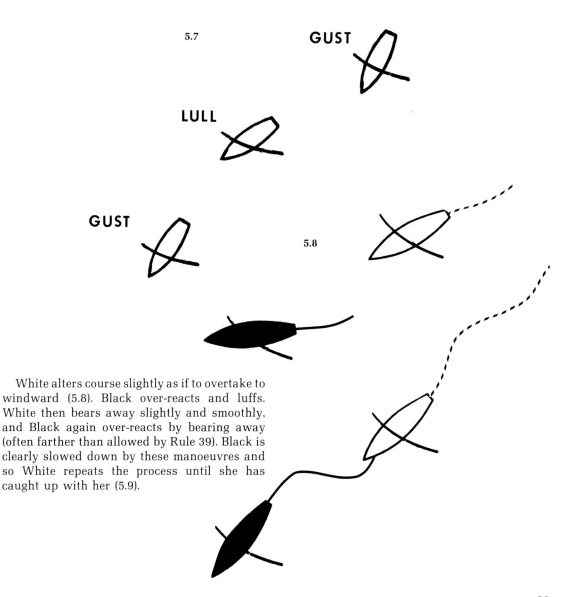

5.7

5.8

White alters course slightly as if to overtake to windward (5.8). Black over-reacts and luffs. White then bears away slightly and smoothly, and Black again over-reacts by bearing away (often farther than allowed by Rule 39). Black is clearly slowed down by these manoeuvres and so White repeats the process until she has caught up with her (5.9).

5.9

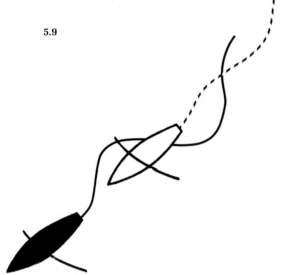

When White is within half a length or so of Black, she repeats the dummy pass to windward, taking care not to luff too high (5.10). As Black responds by luffing herself, White dips below her stern and passes to leeward. As she does so she shouts 'Don't bear away!' By the time Black has regained her composure and her proper course White will probably be through her wind shadow.

5.10

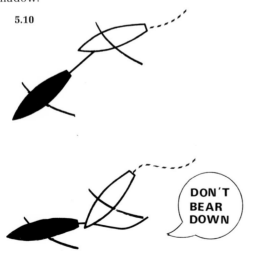

White then hardens up to her proper course and uses the increase in speed to pull ahead of Black (5.11). Even if she does not succeed in getting clear ahead she at least has an overlap to leeward and so the right to the inside berth at the gybe mark. This in itself is enough to give her the lead at the start of the next leg.

5.11

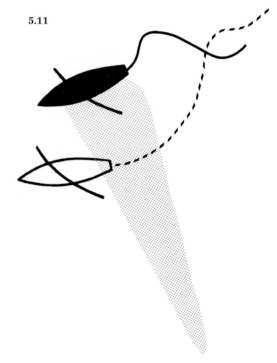

5.212 Overtaking to windward
This does not guarantee the inside berth at the mark, but on a long reach it may be preferable to try to pass on the windward side and get clear ahead than to go to leeward and get stuck in a wind shadow.

White, chasing, decides to pass to windward and so starts to harden up when at least a length behind Black. If Black starts to luff up, White converts her tactics to those of Section 5.211 and passes her to leeward. It is almost never worthwhile to get involved in a luffing match.

However, Black does not luff and so White sails as fast as possible until abeam of Black (5.12). She should be far enough away so that if Black should decide to luff, White will be able to call 'Mast abeam' before Black could hit her. In this way all of Black's luffs will be quickly curtailed and a luffing match prevented. Once she is abeam of Black, White starts to bear away on to her proper course thus keeping Black in her wind shadow as long as possible, and sails into the lead.

5.22 Defence Against an Opponent

There is no way of slowing down an opponent who is chasing you. White, ahead, ignores Black and sails her own course as fast as possible – looking forward at the waves and the next mark and not back at Black. White sails slightly low of her proper course to discourage Black from attempting to pass to leeward: this is especially important near the mark when such action would give Black water for the mark. If Black does decide to go to leeward there is nothing White can do other than sail faster. However, she should try to stay as low as she can get away with so that as the mark approaches she will have to harden up and may be able to break Black's overlap (see Section 6.3).

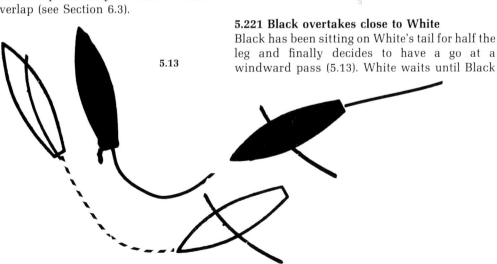

5.12

5.13

5.221 Black overtakes close to White

Black has been sitting on White's tail for half the leg and finally decides to have a go at a windward pass (5.13). White waits until Black has a reasonable overlap and then luffs violently, right up to closehauled or even head-to-wind. If Black actually succeeds in avoiding a collision she will in any case be suitably shaken and is unlikely to try that again. White just as quickly resumes her course with the minimum loss of speed and distance (5.14).

By waiting for the overlap, White stopped Black from escaping the luff by dipping to leeward.

5.14

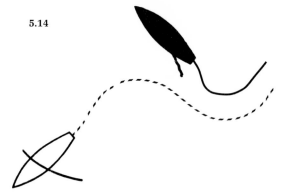

5.222 Black overtakes far away from White

White's tactics here depend on whether Black is her only opponent or there are others nearby. Unless it is crucial that Black be beaten, White cannot afford to indulge in a luffing match with Black and would do better to let her pass than to lose six places on the reach while trying to defend herself.

However, if Black is the only enemy, then White must aim to keep herself between Black and the next mark (5.15). This will inevitably result in sailing well above the proper course, but if carried out correctly Black will be unable to overtake. White must watch out for any sign that Black might try to pass to leeward instead, and react accordingly to try to discourage the idea.

5.223 The luffing match

Again it must be stressed that luffing matches often lose places rather than save them. Here, Black is overtaking White from a distance, and

5.15

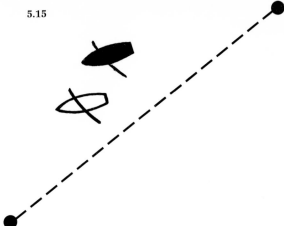

on the windward side. White responds with a luff. But Black is too far ahead and so curtails the luff (5.16).

5.16

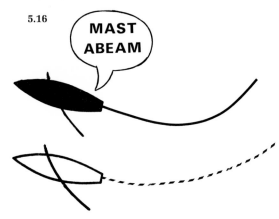

White is required to bear away to her proper course and cannot luff again until the overlap is broken (Rule 38.2). To regain her luffing rights, she bears away hard (5.17). Since the overlap is determined by a line at right angles to her own stern, she has now broken the overlap and is free to luff again as necessary.

This time White luffs slowly, just enough to keep herself between the mark and Black (see diagram 5.15), since a rapid luff would quickly be curtailed by Black again.

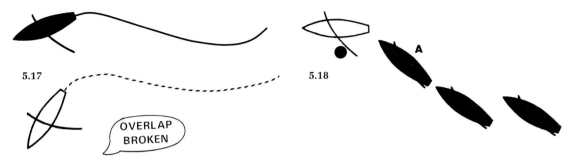

5.17

5.18

OVERLAP
BROKEN

5.3 SAILING WITH A GROUP

5.31 White in the Lead

After rounding the upwind mark the fleet fans out with some boards sailing high and some low. The main danger to White is from those that sail low and so manage to establish an overlap to leeward and a claim for water at the next mark. However, White's nearest opponent is A who is almost certain to try to pass to windward (5.18). This poses no danger to White unless A manages to take her wind. Therefore White should sail as low as possible as a defence against those sailing low, but when necessary luffing up slightly to ensure staying in clean air. Above all, White

must stay calm and should concentrate on her technique and the wind and waves, and not on how close those behind her are!

Occasionally a specific defence against a particularly troublesome opponent may be needed. This is discussed in Section 5.22.

5.32 White in the Middle

On rounding the first mark White may try to pass either to leeward or to windward of the leaders (5.19). The advantage of sailing low is that she may be able to claim water for the next mark even if she has only a small overlap on the board ahead of her. The disadvantage is that she will probably be sailing in air that has been cut

5.19

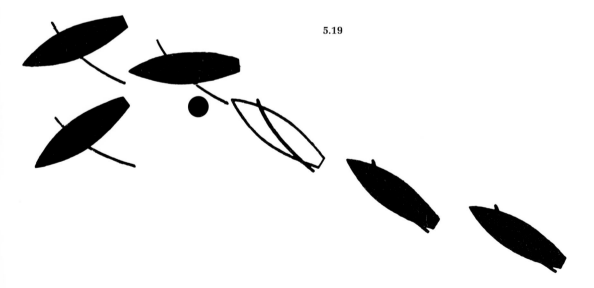

5.20

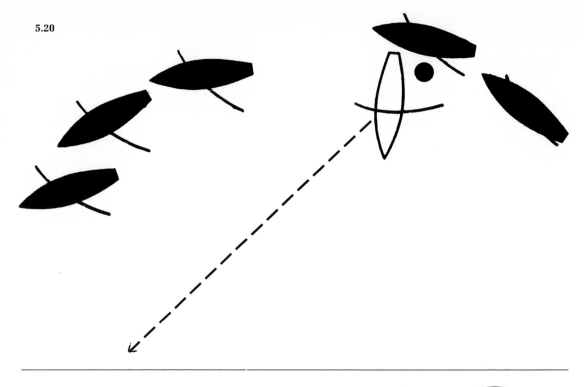

5.21

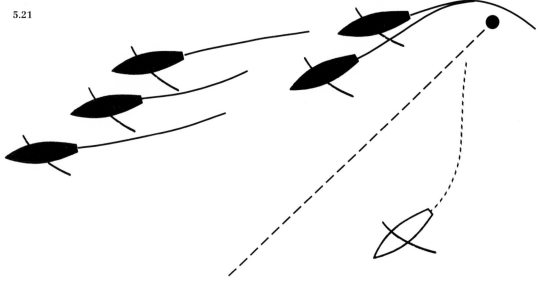

up by those sailing high. If she sails high she will of course have clean air, but she may end up on the outside of the group at the next mark. Which course to take depends on the conditions at the time – which way is the tide flowing? will a wind shift turn the reach into a close fetch? – and on which way the boards ahead are going.

5.321 The leaders sail high

White sees that the leaders are sailing high (5.20). There is no tide to provide a reason for doing so. On rounding the upwind mark, therefore, White sails very low. By doing this she stops anyone else from sailing below her, which would restrict her freedom, and also ensures that she is clear of the wind shadows of those sailing high. If she let anyone sail to leeward of her she would be unable to bear away far enough to avoid the dirty wind, and would end up last.

Having cleared her air, White concentrates on sailing fast and as close to the proper course as possible (5.21). By doing this she will often end up sailing a shorter course than the leaders, and going faster! However, about halfway down the reach it will appear that those up to windward are gaining on her (5.22). This is because they are sailing closer to the wind and thus faster. When they finally reach the wing mark they will have to

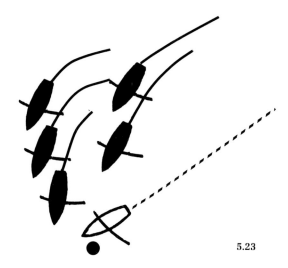

5.23

bear away onto a broad reach while White sails in fast from below with the inside berth (5.23). Here, White will see how much she has gained.

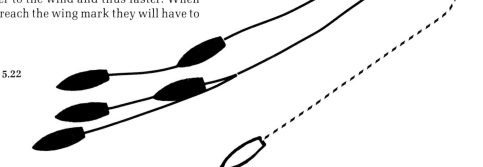

5.22

This tactic is particularly effective when the tide is flowing upwind since the boards that sail high are likely to end up sailing much higher than they expected. Once this tactic has been started it must be continued to the end: bailing out halfway down the leg inevitably leads to disaster since the gain is usually made right at the end.

5.322 The leaders sail low

Much less common, this situation usually occurs when there is a strong downwind tide. White sees what is happening and so sails high, keeping as close to her proper course as possible (5.24).

5.33 White at the Back of the Group

In this situation White is attempting to pass the whole group rather than just one or two boards.

She should almost always sail well to leeward of the rest of the bunch, keeping clear of their dirty wind. Spectacular gains can be made.

5.24

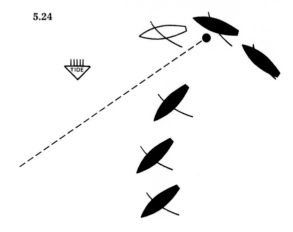

6
The Wing Mark

Tactics are the same for port and starboard hand courses.

6.1 ROUNDING ALONE

As with all marks the turn should be started before reaching the mark. White starts her turn before the mark and on rounding leaves the mark on her proper course (6.1).

Black rounds after she has reached the mark, sails about two lengths farther than White, and ends up below her proper course – which could be embarrassing if the next leg turns out to be a close fetch and Black has to tack up to the mark!

6.2 MARK-ROUNDING WITH ONE OPPONENT

Rule 42 of the Racing Rules (Rounding or Passing Marks and Obstructions) is often regarded as one of the more difficult to understand. However, in practice it usually means that the person who claims his rights first, even if too early, will have the easier case to prove at protest. The secret to using this Rule is to leave the call late enough so that it is not blatantly premature, but yet to call early enough that the other board does not call first.

6.21 Establishing An Overlap

(i) As the mark is neared, White should if at all possible establish an overlap on Black. White

rides the waves in any direction just to gain the overlap. As soon as she has her bow ahead of a line at right angles to Black's stern (6.2), White

6.1

6.2

sails for the mark trying to keep her overlap until she feels she can safely call for water.

White should call for water at about four board lengths from the mark, but she must remember that Black can break the overlap until Black is two lengths from the mark (6.3). The reason for calling early is that it is then up to Black to prove that she broke the overlap in time. If White leaves it too long then Black will call 'No water'. It is then much harder for White to prove that she had gained an overlap before the two lengths circle, even if she had in fact done so in plenty of time.

6.3

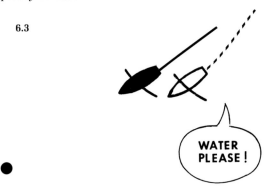

Once she has reached the two lengths circle with her overlap intact White has the right to round the mark inside of Black, even if the overlap is then broken.

(ii) Often Black will be approaching the wing mark from above the rhumb line, while White

has followed the tactics of Chapter 5 by sailing along the proper course (6.4). In this situation White can claim an overlap much earlier than in *(i)* since the overlap depends on a line at right angles to Black's stern. If at all possible, White should claim the overlap.

6.4

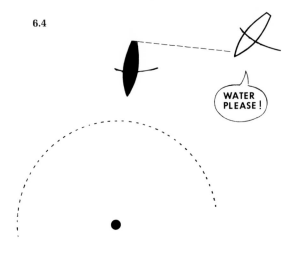

Often Black will still reach the mark ahead of White, and although required to give room to White, White is not close enough to insist and so Black rounds ahead (6.5). However, since Black will be sailing slower on a broad reach than

6.5

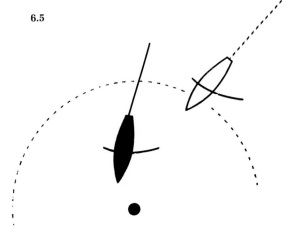

White on a beam reach, White may well be in a position to insist (6.6), and in such a case it is important that she had made her claim in sufficient time (Rule 42.1 d).

6.6

6.7

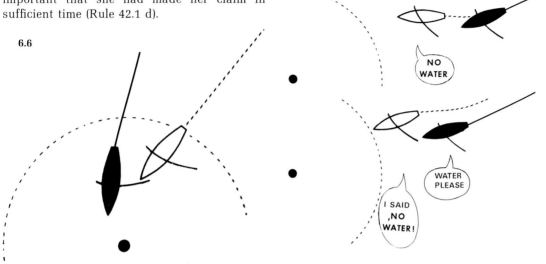

NO WATER

WATER PLEASE

I SAID ,NO WATER!

6.22 Preventing An Overlap

It is better to prevent an overlap than to break one that has already been established. In preventing one it is up to the challenger to prove that she has created it in sufficient time. In breaking one it is the leader's onus of proof to show that the overlap was broken in time.

White sees Black coming up fast from behind (6.7). To avoid having to give her water at the next mark, White luffs up before reaching the two length limit. This has the effect of moving the line across her stern forward of Black, thus denying her an overlap. It is important that White informs Black of the situation.

If it is done well before the mark, Black may still establish a legal overlap after White has called 'No water'. However, if White still insists on her first call (6.7 below), then Black's only option is to concede to White and protest. Unless there are plenty of witnesses it will be difficult for Black to win her case in all but the most blatantly clear-cut situations.

6.23 Breaking an Overlap

Often an overlap will be impossible to break. Occasionally, however, in fresh winds with large waves the overlap will be on and off throughout the length of the leg as first White and then Black

6.8

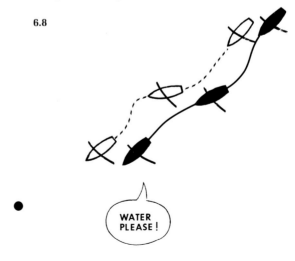

WATER PLEASE !

catches a wave and accelerates. In these conditions both may have difficulty in proving their claim and, at protest, it will probably be decided in favour of Black (the follower) unless White can convince the jury that she successfully attempted to break the overlap at the two length limit. She can do this by luffing up just before the two-lengths circle, so bringing her stern line forward of Black. She must shout (6.9). Once the overlap has been convincingly broken White rounds the mark normally and Black must keep clear.

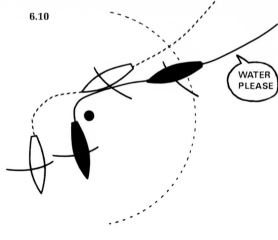

6.10

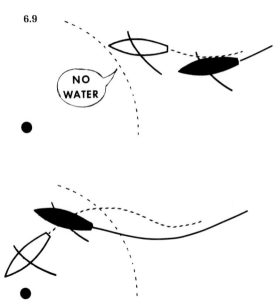

6.9

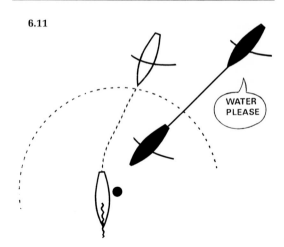

6.11

6.24 Breaking an Overlap Inside the Two-lengths Circle

Usually, when the overlap is broken inside the circle White (leading) still has to give Black room at the mark (6.10).

However, sometimes White gets to the mark, having conceded water to Black, only to find that she can round it clearly ahead of Black (6.11). Obviously White does just that, rather than wait for Black.

6.3 ROUNDING IN A GROUP

A is clear ahead and rounds in the lead (6.12). B has an overlap on C who has an overlap on D who is within two lengths of the mark. Therefore both B and C call for water and round the mark as shown (6.13). The result is that B ends up to windward and possibly ahead of C and D, in an ideal position for the next leg. This shows the importance of getting an overlap if at all possible.

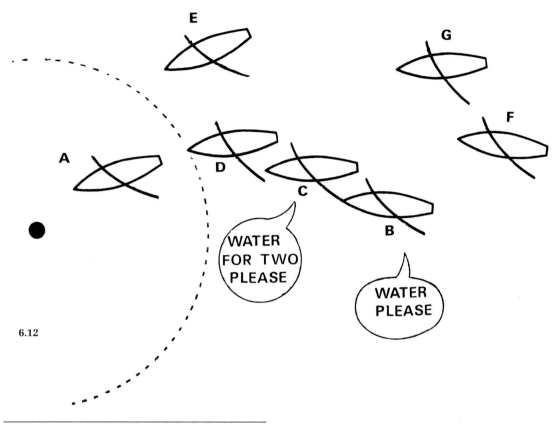

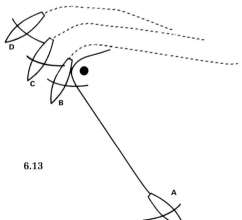

E has a choice. She may sail round on the outside of D and into a disastrous position for the next reach (6.14). Alternatively, she slows down slightly and crosses behind all the others (but not F or G) to round close to the mark, just

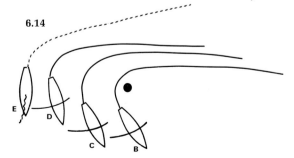

behind B (6.15). Often, because of crowding, B will do a poor job rounding and so E will be able to sail through onto B's windward quarter. E is then well positioned to sail the next reach with the prospect of claiming an overlap at the next mark from B.

6.15

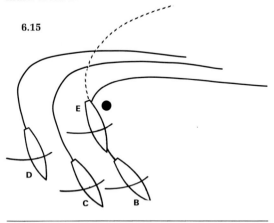

F does not have water on the leaders, but does on G. She therefore does a perfect rounding to close up with E (6.16), and G goes round beneath F.

The boards in the group start the second reach in the positions shown in (6.17). The points to notice are that:

1 A has increased her lead considerably because C and D were slowed down by having to round outside of B.
2 B has come from fifth to second simply because she established an overlap on C.
3 E has changed a disastrous position into a promising one.

6.16

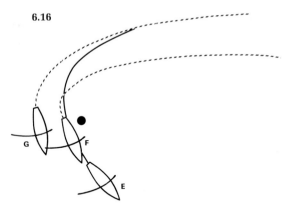

6.17

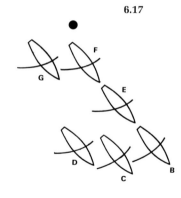

7

The Second Reach

On the second reaching leg it is the boards up to windward that will be able to claim an overlap, and so claim an inside berth, at the leeward mark. Because of this the tactics on this leg are slightly different to those of the previous leg. The strength and direction of the tide must still be borne in mind when deciding how to sail this leg, and again when starting the second reach a transit on the shore should be lined up with the leeward mark if at all possible. If sailing alone White's general strategy is identical to that for the first reach, as described in Section 5.1. The general principles of overtaking an opponent are also the same as those in Section 5.21.

7.1 SAILING WITH ONE OPPONENT

7.11 White Leads Black

White rounds the reaching mark just ahead of Black. Black will almost certainly try to overtake White to windward so as to gain the inside berth at the next mark. To try to prevent this White sails high after rounding the mark before she assumes her proper course (7.1 left).

If White does not luff up on rounding the mark, Black should indeed try to pass to windward (7.1 right).

However, if White does luff, as she has done here, then Black will realise that she is likely to be luffed if she tries to pass her to windward. So,

as soon as she sees that White is sailing high, Black dips down to leeward. Black is then to leeward of White and clear of her wind shadow.

Both boards now concentrate on sailing fast for the next mark. White has an inherent advantage because she was ahead of Black at the start of the reach, and is also to windward of her. Despite this, Black is likely to lose less distance by sailing her own course to leeward of White, even if she does not actually beat White to the mark, than if she tries to pass her to windward and ends up in a luffing match. This is especially important if there are other opponents ahead to be caught.

7.1

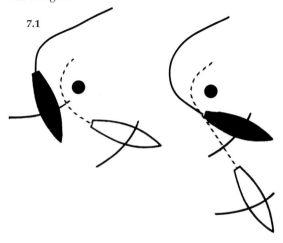

As the two boards approach the leeward mark their relative positions will have to be re-assessed. Black may find herself ahead of White, in which case she rounds the mark in the lead, or she may be level with or behind White. The tactics for all these positions are discussed in Chapter 8.

7.12 Black is Behind White, but has an Inside Overlap

As soon as they are clear of the mark, White tries to persuade Black to go to leeward of her by luffing (7.2).

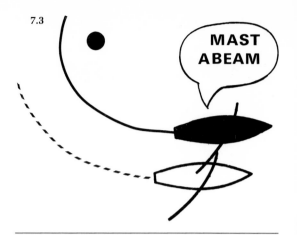

7.3

MAST ABEAM

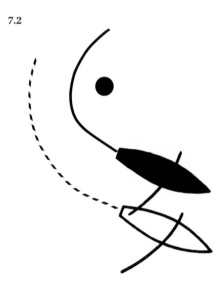

7.2

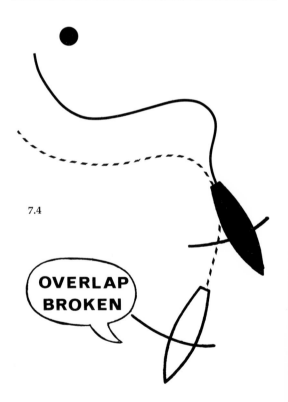

7.4

OVERLAP BROKEN

Black will have to respond to the luff because her overlap prevents her from ducking down to leeward. She luffs with White (7.3) and if at all possible calls 'Mast abeam' (Rule 38.4).

The moment that Black calls 'Mast abeam' White bears away (7.4). If she bears away sharply she may break Black's overlap and so regain luffing rights. By doing this she will also place herself far to leeward of Black and so in

little danger of being blanketed by her. White then sails the rest of the leg as fast as possible, ignoring Black's presence until near the leeward mark when she can reconsider her position.

If she can do so White must bear away onto her proper course and Black has safely established herself to windward of White (7.5). Black then sails as fast as possible to overtake White to windward. Even if she fails to do so she will probably still have the inside berth at the next mark.

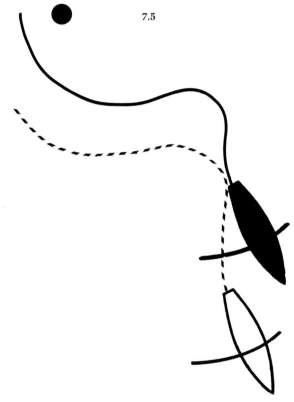

7.5

If Black cannot call 'Mast abeam' then she must decide whether to continue to attempt to overtake to windward, with the advantage that has with regard to the inside position at the next mark, or whether to go to leeward which avoids the risk of a lengthy luffing match. The technique of overtaking on a reach has been described in Section 5.21.

7.13 Black has the Inside Berth, Level or Ahead of White

Black starts the second reach to windward of White (7.6), and if she maintains her position will have the inside berth at the next mark too. White's only hope is to sail a course off to leeward, well clear of Black's wind shadow. Black anticipates White's strategy and so sails her own proper course so that White is forced to sail a longer distance. In spite of this, all is not lost for White. As she approaches the mark she should re-evaluate her position and act accordingly (see next Chapter), and she may still be able to beat Black around the leeward mark.

7.6

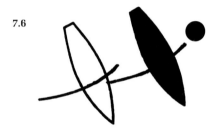

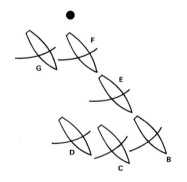

6.17

99

7.2 SAILING WITH A GROUP

In Section 6.2 we discussed rounding the wing mark in a group. The position of the boards at the end of the Section was that shown in (6.17), also on page 99. Here we will consider the tactics for the second reaching leg for these same boards.

A is clear ahead, and so she sails her own proper course. B is being threatened by E who is trying to pass her to windward. If E manages to get an overlap to windward of B she will have the right to water at the next mark. To discourage E from achieving this B sails slightly high, above her proper course (7.7). If B sails too high she will risk letting C and D through.

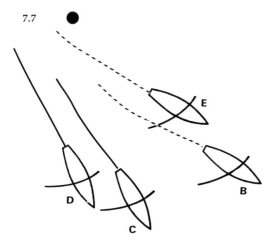

If it looks like E will overtake to windward, B luffs sharply and then quickly regains her course. If done quickly and high, such a luff will probably discourage E from trying again. A slow luff is much more likely to let E claim 'Mast abeam' and so establish herself to windward of B, as well as taking all of them too far upwind of the proper course – letting C and D through to take second and third places.

If at the end of the leg E has a small overlap B may well be able to break it and so deny E the right to water for the mark. Just before the two-length limit is reached B bears away sharply, bringing the line through her stern forward of E

and breaking the overlap (7.8). Having done so, B shouts out 'Overlap broken – No water!' and rounds the mark ahead of her. (See also the next Chapter.)

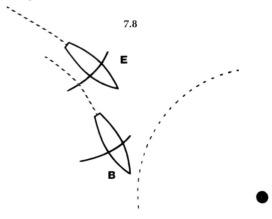

C should try to sail her own course, keeping clear of B's wind shadow. Unfortunately she may be prevented from bearing away as far as she wants to by D who is sailing below her (7.9). If

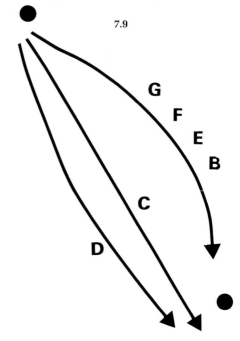

that happens there is little that she can do other than sail as fast as possible. D has no one below her and so can sail low enough to stay in clean air. Because B will be sailing high, D and C may find that they sail a shorter course to the mark than B.

E will try to establish an overlap to windward of B. If B luffs violently then E should either try to overtake B at a greater distance from her, so that B cannot luff her effectively, or she should stay as close as possible to her windward quarter, without trying to overtake, until near the next mark (7.10). By doing either of these E will be

7.10

able to defend herself against F in the same way that B is defending herself against E. For E to try to go to leeward would be suicide, since she would probably end up stuck below B and F while being unable to clear her air because of C and D below her.

F uses the same tactics as E, since she also has someone ahead of her (E) and someone behind her (G). Unfortunately, if B decides to luff E then F will also have to respond (7.10). Again, to go to leeward would achieve nothing.

G has a free choice of whether to sail high to gain an overlap on F, or to sail low to try to overtake the whole group (see diagram 6.17, page 99). Unless she is convinced that she can overtake the whole fleet she should not attempt a leeward course. If she does go to leeward but does not come out ahead, she will find herself rounding the mark outside all the others. Even those boards that do not have any right to an inside berth will take one since G will be unable to stop them.

SUMMARY

A   sails the proper course to the leeward mark

B, E, F, G all sail high to defend themselves against those behind, and to attack those ahead.

C, D sail low to keep in clean air, and to try to sail a shorter course than B and the others.

8
The Leeward Mark, from a Reach

8.1 ROUNDING ALONE

The leg after this mark is a beat to windward. The difference, therefore, between rounding the leeward mark well or badly rests not just on the speed of rounding but also on whether any ground is lost to leeward after rounding.

RIGHT

White approaches the mark about two lengths wide of the rhumb line (8.1). She then starts her turn *before* reaching the mark so that she has finished turning by the time she actually reaches it. She then skims the mark while already on a closehauled course.

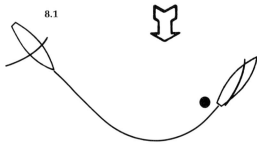

WRONG

Black, however, thinks that if she passes close to the buoy she has made a good turn (8.2). By doing this she cannot start her manoeuvre until *after* she has passed the mark, and so ends up two lengths farther downwind than White.

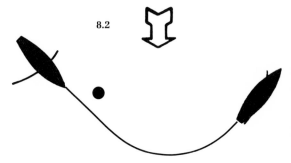

This time (8.3) Black approaches the mark correctly, but does not start her turn until level with the mark and again finishes up downwind of where she should be.

Both times Black sails about four lengths farther than White, since she first sails past the mark and then has to sail back up to it just to get

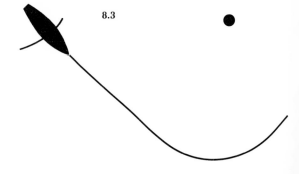

back to the level she should have been at had she rounded well.

Timing the turn to round a mark well requires a lot of practice, and it is very easy to be persuaded to round as Black has done when there are other sailors around who are reluctant to give you sufficient room to round well. Do not be intimidated: if entitled to room then demand plenty of it.

The daggerboard will often have been pulled out or retracted for reaching. It is crucial that it is returned to the correct position for the beat well before starting to turn. The most disastrous thing that can happen is to round the mark with your daggerboard only half down and then slide downwind onto those who have rounded outside you!

8.2 ROUNDING WITH ONE OPPONENT

8.21 White Clear Ahead
Both boards round the mark perfectly (8.4). As she rounds the mark White luffs up high, momentarily. Black is then forced to sail on, under White's leeward quarter (8.5). White then bears away again without having lost any speed and resumes a closehauled course, thus effectively covering Black.

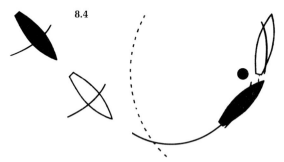

8.4

This is a disastrous position for Black, since she is fully in White's wind shadow. Black tacks off as soon as possible to clear her air. If it is early in the race and Black is not a major opponent, White ignores her and sails her own course.

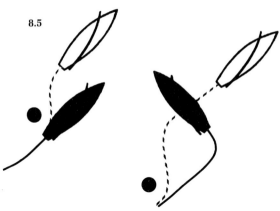

8.5

However, if Black must be beaten then White tries to prevent her from tacking off by staying so close to her that she does not have enough room to tack. (Tactics for close covering have been discussed in Section 3.222.)

Black must clear her wind, so she can either try sailing free and fast to try to break through to

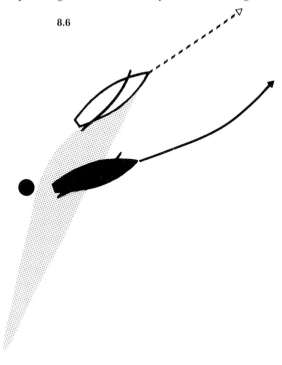

8.6

leeward (8.6), or she can try slowing down and bearing away to create room in which to tack (8.7). (Breaking cover is also in Section 3.222.)

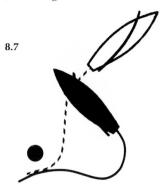

8.7

8.22 Black Claims an Overlap on White

White may or may not have luffing rights (see Rule 38): if she does not, she can try to regain them by bearing away sharply before reaching the two-length limit (8.8). As the overlap is broken she calls out 'Overlap broken – no water!'. Black is then forced to follow White around the mark.

If this does not work and Black maintains her overlap, White will have to round the mark wide

leaving Black enough room to round inside her (8.9). Having rounded the mark White will find that she is no longer ahead of Black. Their tactics will then follow those given in Section 3.223.

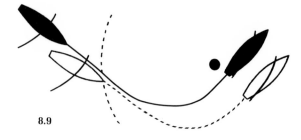

8.9

On the other hand, if White does have luffing rights she can then ensure that she rounds the mark first by luffing Black before reaching the two-length limit. There are two ways of doing this, depending on how much of an overlap Black has. Should Black have only a small overlap, then White luffs very sharply, just before the limit (8.10). She luffs as high and quickly as possible, and then just as quickly returns to her proper course, or perhaps even lower. If done quickly and suddenly, without warning, this will usually break the overlap and allow White to round first.

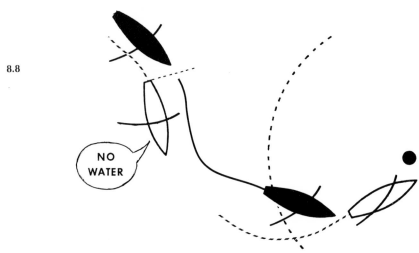

8.8

NO WATER

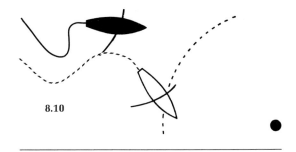

8.10

White is now ahead of Black and so on rounding the mark (8.11) will luff up slightly (Section 8.21).

But if Black has a greater overlap she is likely to be able to curtail all but the most gentle of luffs with a call of 'Mast abeam', so such a violent luff would not work. Instead, White steers a gentle luff before the two-length limit, making sure that she shouts out her intention to luff Black to the wrong side of the mark (8.12). White then sails

8.11

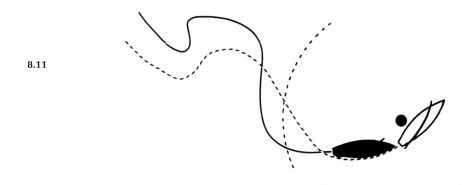

8.12

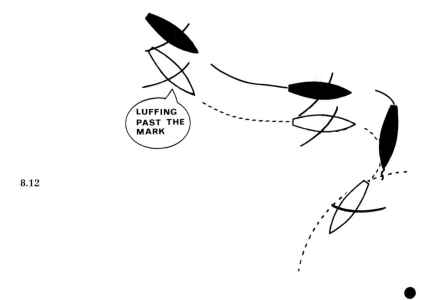

Black past the mark until White is confident that she can break the overlap when she bears away for it or until Black escapes from the luff.

Black does this either by tacking away, which obviously loses a lot of ground (8.13), or by slowing down until she can duck under White's stern.

8.13

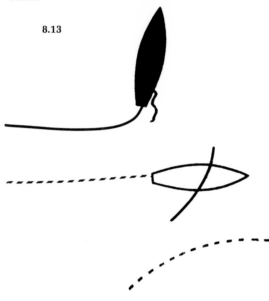

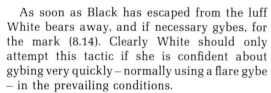

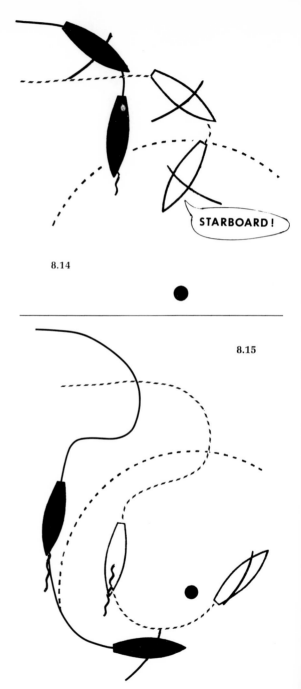

8.14

8.15

As soon as Black has escaped from the luff White bears away, and if necessary gybes, for the mark (8.14). Clearly White should only attempt this tactic if she is confident about gybing very quickly – normally using a flare gybe – in the prevailing conditions.

White will then have to gybe again to round the mark (8.15). Black follows suit. White rounds first, luffing up as before.

However, because of all these rapid manoeuvres White may find herself doing a poor rounding. Black seizes the opportunity and rounds well, crossing White's stern to end up inside on her windward quarter (8.16). Black's tactics are then as those of White in Section 3.224.

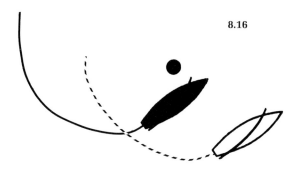

8.16

However, White can encourage Black to round badly by crowding her. As we saw at the beginning of this Chapter, Black must approach the mark wide in order to round it well. White tries to prevent this by giving Black little room as she comes up to the mark. Black then rounds badly and White, who has necessarily approached wide, rounds well, crossing Black's stern to sail through onto her windward quarter.

8.24 Black Leads with an Inside Overlap

White attempts to gain an inside overlap by luffing up and crossing Black's stern (8.18). Except on close reaches this will usually result in an increase in speed which White uses to drive through to an overlap before reaching the two-length limit.

Black defends herself from the attack by also luffing up, so stopping White from crossing her stern.

8.23 Boards Level but More than One Length Apart

Any attempt by White to luff Black as they approach the mark would fail before it even started. White's only hope of beating Black to the mark depends on Black making a poor rounding (8.17). If Black rounds well, then White has to round outside her and ends up in a hopeless position.

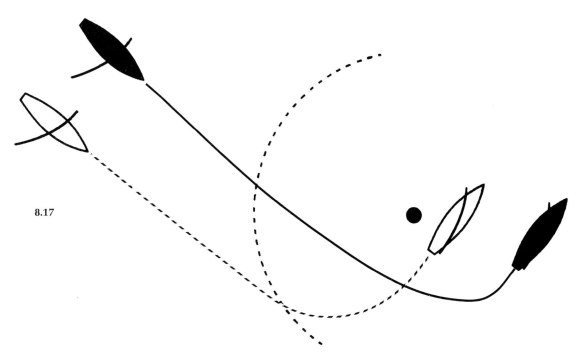

8.17

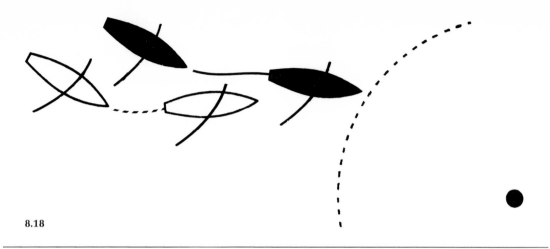

8.18

White realizes that Black has successfully countered her attack and so she bears away for the mark (8.19). Having successfully kept her inside berth, Black immediately bears away also.

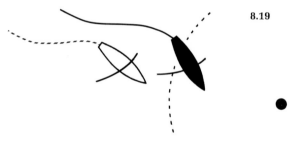

8.19

However, all is not lost for White. All these manoeuvres have taken place fairly close to the leeward mark, and by the time she has sorted herself out Black may find that she is too close to it to round well. If she rounds badly, White slips through the gap to end up on Black's windward quarter (8.20, above). By now both boards are pretty close to the mark, and Black must ensure that she does not get rushed into a disastrous rounding (8.20, below).

8.3 ROUNDING IN A GROUP
In this Section we will consider groups of only three boards, for the sake of simplicity.

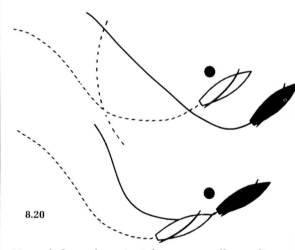

8.20

Nevertheless, the principles are equally applicable to groups of any size, and indeed the larger the group the greater are the possibilities for gaining a lot of places.

8.31 All Boards are Overlapping

8.311 Outside board leads
White's tactics

If White does not have luffing rights she should try to regain them by bearing away sharply to break Black's overlap. It is advisable to call out that the overlap has been broken. Should White be unable to break the overlap then she has to round the mark as best as she can, leaving enough room for Grey and Black to round it well also (8.21). Unfortunately, the inside one (Black) often does a bad rounding and loses a lot of ground for the group.

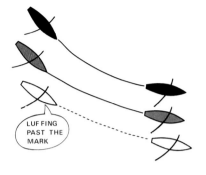

8.22

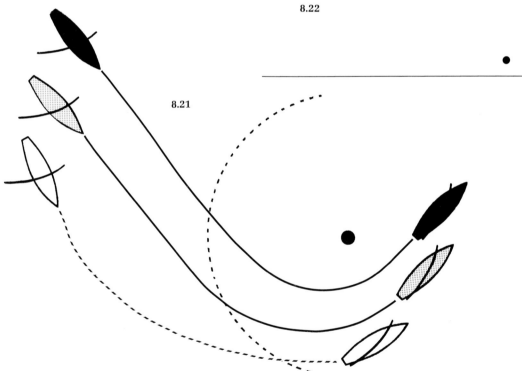

8.21

On the other hand, if White has, or can acquire, luffing rights on all those to windward of her (Rule 38.6) then she is in a good position to luff the whole group to the wrong side of the mark (8.22). She must shout out that she is doing so.

White continues the luff until one of four things happens:

(i) White has luffed the group far enough that she can break the overlap by bearing away, with or without a gybe, for the mark (8.23). Black and Grey will follow, but White then denies them water.

(ii) Black escapes by doing a quick flare gybe across the others' sterns (8.24). White then has to decide whether to abandon the luff, possibly

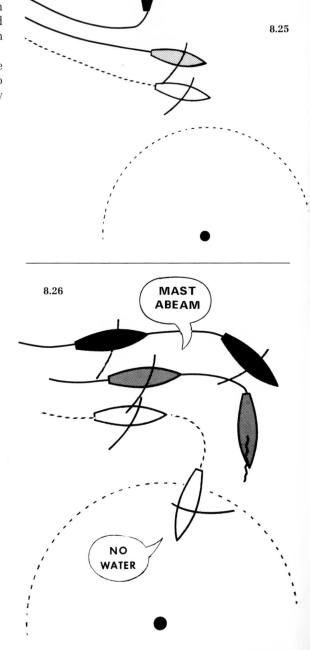

8.25

8.23

8.26

MAST ABEAM

NO WATER

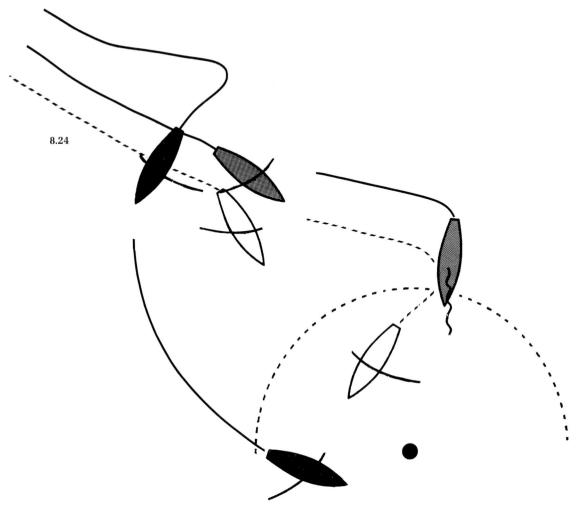

8.24

without managing to break Grey's overlap, in order to consolidate her rights over Black, or whether to continue the luff a bit further, until she is sure she can shake off Grey. However, by the time she does bear away for the mark she may have lost her overlap on Black.

Ideally, White will be able to bear away immediately, to keep her overlap on Black and also to break Grey's overlap.

(iii) Black tacks away (8.25). However, by doing so she loses so much ground that White can

ignore her and continue the luff until she is sure that she has beaten Grey.

(iv) If either Grey or Black calls 'Mast abeam' on White, then of course White must abandon her luff, hoping to manage to break Grey's overlap anyway (8.26). Should Black call on Grey to curtail her luff, then White is under no obligation to stop luffing as long as she still has luffing rights over Black (and Grey).

Having thus gained the inside berth White must still round the mark well, otherwise she stands to lose all she has gained. It is easy to be crowded into the mark, making a perfect rounding impossible.

Grey's tactics

Grey has the choice of either settling for middle place as they round the mark (see diagram 8.21), or of ignoring White and luffing Black to break her overlap (8.27). By doing this she will probably, although not necessarily, lose her rights over White.

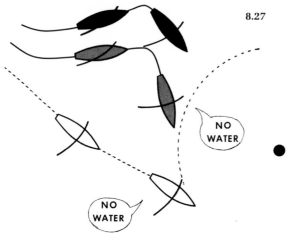

8.27

Grey then does an expert rounding behind White (8.28). The relative positions have been

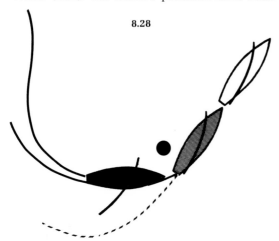

8.28

reversed and Grey is in a better position to tack off for clean air.

Black's tactics

Having established her right to the inside berth at the mark, Black plays a passive role merely making sure that she does have enough water in which to do a perfect rounding.

Should White decide to luff the whole group, Black tries either to curtail the luff with a call of 'Mast abeam' as soon as she is in that position relative to White (not Grey), or she tries to duck out of the luff. It is best to delay this until the luff is well under way, otherwise Black is likely to end up on the outside at the mark (see diagram 8.24).

8.312 Inside board leads

Black's tactics

Black leads with the inside berth (8.29). All she needs to do is round well, leaving no room for White or Grey to slip through. Should Grey try to luff across her stern to gain an overlap, Black can afford to luff slightly to prevent her from succeeding (8.30). Black then quickly returns to her proper course, still having an overlap on White.

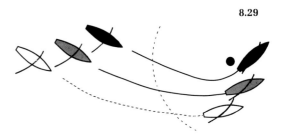

8.29

Grey's tactics

If the wind and waves are suitable, Grey may be able to pick up enough speed by luffing across Black's stern to carry her through into an overlap before the two-lengths limit (see also Section 8.24). If this does not succeed then Grey hopes that Black will do a bad rounding, leaving a gap to slip through (8.31).

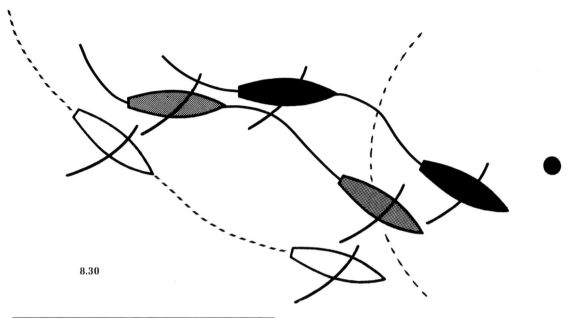

8.30

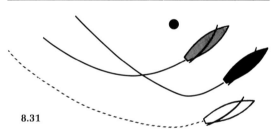

8.31

White's tactics

White may try the tactics just described for Grey (although not at the same time as Grey) to try to improve her position vis-a-vis her. Because of Black's position, Grey is unable to defend herself against such an attack by White since she cannot luff her unless she slows down slightly, which would make it even easier for White to establish herself to windward of Grey (8.32). If

8.32

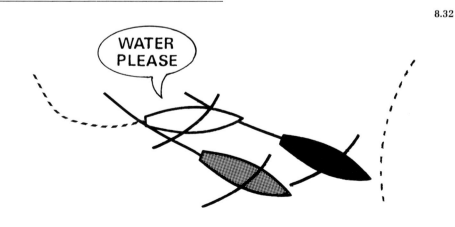

this is unsuccessful, then at least White can follow Black around the mark rather than have to sail round it outside Grey.

Of course, should Black round badly then White can slip into the gap next to the mark to get into a very advantageous position (8.33).

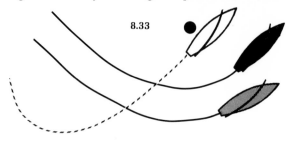

8.33

If Grey also goes for the gap left by Black, then White will either have to follow behind Grey (8.34), or if she did manage to get her overlap on Grey then she will go first, squeezing Grey out into a hopeless position (8.35).

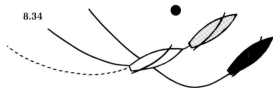

8.34

8.313 Boards level
Black and Grey have little option in this position, in which all three boards are approaching the

downwind mark with their bows level. Black concentrates on rounding well without losing any ground to windward and Grey is forced to round outside her.

White, having no one below her, can sail slightly wide and also slow down so that she can cross their sterns as they round. If Black takes the mark well, then White follows close on her stern (8.36). But if Black rounds poorly, White can seize the opportunity (8.37). In both cases White has considerably improved her position.

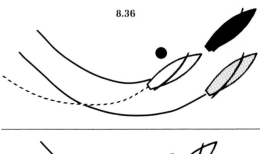

8.36

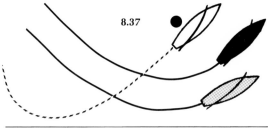

8.37

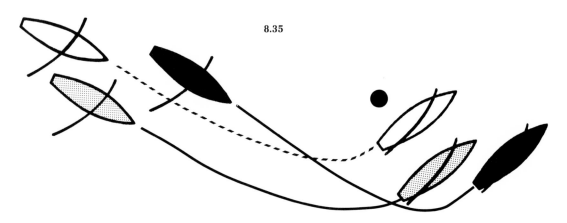

8.35

8.32 Boards not Overlapping

White's tactics

White aims to wind herself between Grey and Black, and then to establish an inside overlap on Black before reaching the two-length limit. She must have luffing rights over Grey, behind her (8.38–9).

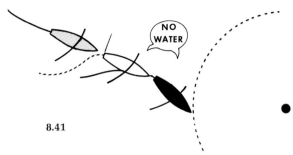

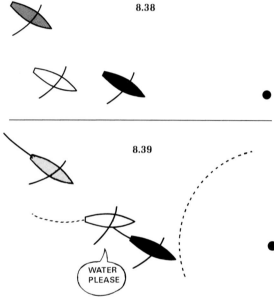

8.38

8.39

If Black responds with a luff, then at least White has placed herself ahead of Grey (8.40). White may have to continue luffing Grey a bit farther until she is sure that she can break Grey's overlap when she bears away (8.41). White then waits for Black to round poorly so that she can improve her position even further.

8.40

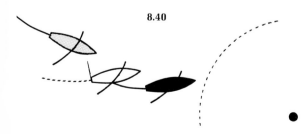

8.41

Should White not have luffing rights over Grey, then there is little that she can do to improve her position except concentrate on rounding as well as possible (8.42).

8.42

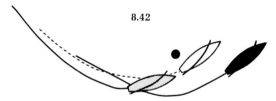

Black's tactics

Black is comfortably in the lead. To maintain her position all she needs to do is to round well, as described at the beginning of this Chapter (8.43). Should White try to cross her stern to gain an overlap, Black can easily defend herself by luffing (see diagram 8.40).

8.43

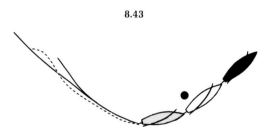

However, Black must make sure that she ends her luff before the two-length limit (8.44), otherwise she may find herself giving away the coveted inside berth rather than protecting it!

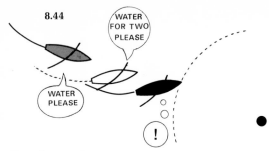

8.44

Grey's tactics

Grey will be trying simply to sail over White, hoping to call 'Mast abeam' on her to prevent the possibility of her wheedling in between Grey and Black. Obviously, if Grey can catch Black she will try to go to windward of her as described in Section 8.21.

If Grey does not succeed in catching up with Black, she satisfies herself with doing a perfect

rounding and slipping through the gap that Black left by her bad rounding (8.45).

8.33 Conclusion

The leeward mark at the end of a reach is often the last one to be rounded before the finish line, and so races can be won or lost there since whoever comes out of the mark first can cover those who round behind or below them.

Rounding successfully in a group requires good technique, a sound working knowledge of the Racing Rules and plenty of confidence. Whenever an opportunity to improve your position presents itself, seize it immediately. Furthermore, most of the tactics discussed in this Chapter need to be executed before reaching the two-length limit, and so you must always be looking ahead and thinking about how to engineer opportunities to round that mark first.

8.45

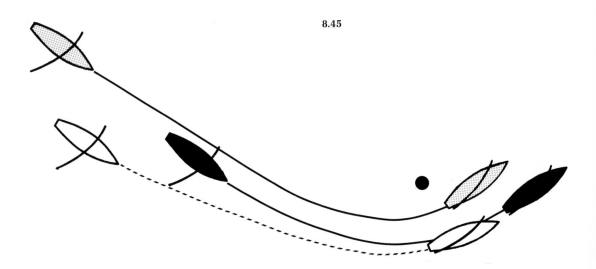

9
The Run

9.1 SAILING ALONE

Having just rounded the windward mark, White locates the leeward mark and as before looks for a transit on shore with which it can be lined up. In light winds with flat water White then sails directly for the mark, keeping the transit in line with it so that she automatically allows for any tidal stream.

In stronger winds, especially when there are reasonably big waves, it is faster to sail a broad reach, surfing down the waves, and then gybe and reach back to the downwind mark. All things being equal, White chooses to start on starboard tack (on a port-hand course) since she will then have to gybe once only. However, on the sea waves are rarely in the same direction as the wind, so White decides to sail on the tack (also called a 'gybe') that allows her to surf the waves in a direction as close to possible to her proper course.

Whichever side of the course White chooses to sail to, the principle is still the same. When she gets a gust and can surf a wave she does so, whatever direction it takes her. Then when the wind drops and she comes off the wave she steers for the mark. In this way she makes full use of the waves and gusts without ending up too far over to one side of the course.

The tack to choose will also be influenced by the direction of the tide. If it is flowing across the wind then White will pick the tack that takes her up-tide first (as in Diagram 9.1). Provided she does this, she will still be able to play the waves to get maximum surfing and speed, without ending the leg too far down-tide of the mark.

Above all, the most important thing to remember is that the run is *not* the time for a rest after sailing the beat. To extract the maximum speed from the board it needs to be continually worked at, and often the run will be more tiring than the beat!

9.2 SAILING WITH ONE OPPONENT

The run differs from other race legs in that it is the board behind that enjoys the possibility of blanketing the one ahead rather than the opposite. This makes it tricky to defend a leading position, but obviously opens up opportunities for the challenger.

White's tactics

White has two ways to attack Black. If she disagrees with the course Black is sailing, she may ignore her and sail her own course as fast as she can. For example, if she feels that Black has under-estimated the strength of the tide, she will sail farther up-tide than Black and so cover a shorter course (9.1).

Also, if there are no particular reasons for choosing one tack rather than the other, then

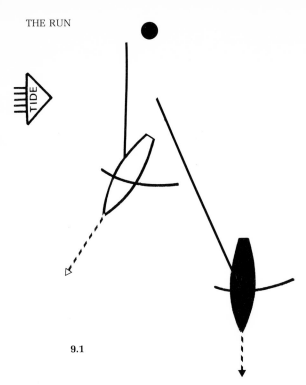

9.1

fast as possible, looking forward and only occasionally glancing back to check that White is not covering her. When she does change course to clear her wind it should be as smoothly as possible and only by as little as is necessary, in order not to lose any speed (9.4).

Finally, she should remember which side the next mark is to be left, and in general should sail to that side of the course in order to discourage White from overlapping her to gain water at the mark. Thus, on a port-hand course Black will tend to sail to the starboard side (looking upwind).

9.21 White Passes to Port: Both on Starboard Tack, Mark to Port

This is the most favourable situation for White. The next mark is to be left to port so both boards will have to gybe at some point before rounding it.

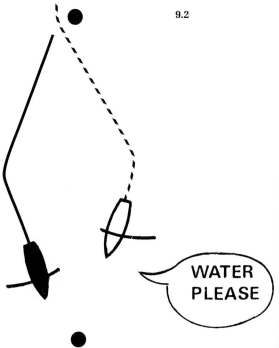

9.2

WATER PLEASE

while Black starts on starboard White decides to gybe into port, thus standing to benefit from an inside berth when they meet at the next mark, if they are racing on a port-hand course (9.2).

Finally, White may decide to overtake Black while staying close to her. To do this she merely follows her precisely, always keeping Black directly downwind. She will gradually catch up with Black, especially if Black panics and loses her concentration (9.3).

Having caught up with Black, White then overlaps her. She will have to decide on which side to overtake: there are eight possibilities which we will discuss below.

Black's tactics

Whatever the relative positions at the start of the leg, Black concentrates on staying out of White's wind shadow while also sailing her own course as fast as possible. She should try not to keep looking back at White, which is guaranteed to ruin her own concentration, but rather sail as

118

9.3

9.4

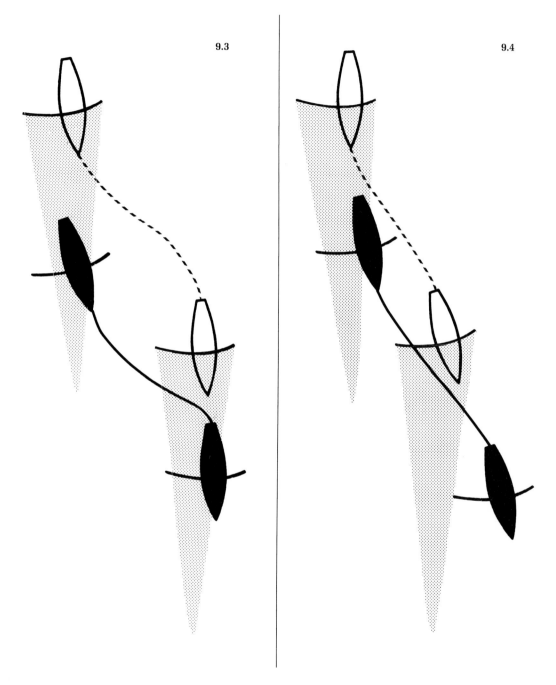

White catches up and overlaps Black on her port side, which is also Black's leeward side (9.5). Therefore White is not in danger of being luffed. Furthermore, if Black gybes then White has right of way since she is still on starboard. White's strategy is, therefore, to continue on starboard at least until she is mast abeam of Black (9.6). She can then gybe, knowing that if Black also gybes White will still have right of way.

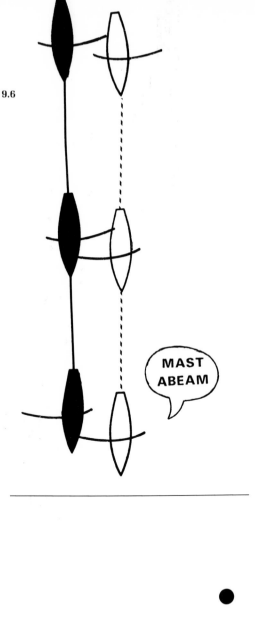

9.6

9.5

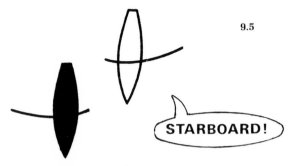

Alternatively, if White cannot achieve the mast abeam position, she continues to sail on starboard until she reaches the point where, if she gybes and luffs up for the mark, she will be able to call 'Mast abeam' (9.7).

9.7

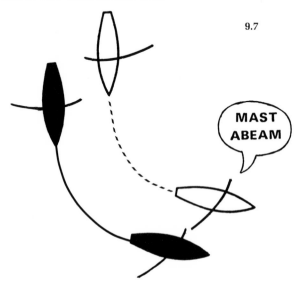

Finally, when they do reach the mark, if White is not already clear ahead she will have the inside berth. Black has no effective defence to White's tactics other than sailing faster than her.

9.22 White Passes to Starboard: Both on Starboard, Mark to Port

Trying to pass an opponent on her starboard side (i.e. to windward, except in a dead run) with the mark to be left to port is incomparably more difficult than passing to port. Not only does White stand to be luffed out of the race, but if she does not succeed in completely overtaking Black then she will have the outside berth at the leeward mark and will lose all that she had gained.

Black's defence is, of course, to luff White (9.8). She can either do this suddenly, hoping to frighten White off or even to hit her (without causing damage), and yet lose little ground while doing so. Or Black can luff gently, just sailing White past the mark until she can gybe for it

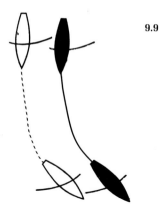

9.9

herself, knowing that she will have the lead and the inside berth when they actually reach the mark (9.9).

Once caught in a luff, White can only escape by either calling 'Mast abeam', for which she actually needs to be ahead of Black, or by slowing down (difficult in strong winds) and crossing over to overtake on the other side as described above (9.10).

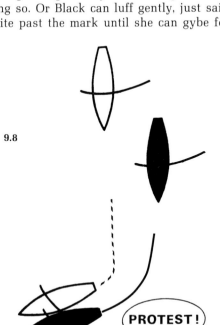

9.8

PROTEST!

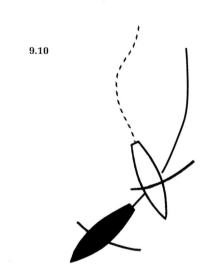

9.10

If White insists on trying to overtake to windward she should do so at a distance from Black so that at least she will not get a sudden vicious luff that might put her out of the race.

At some point both boards will have to gybe to round the mark. If Black gybes close to the mark there is nothing that White can do to improve her position (see diagram 9.9). But if Black gybes at a distance from the mark, then if White has overtaken her sufficiently and is ahead of the mast abeam position as seen by Black (9.11) she has luffing rights as soon as she gybes (Rule 38.3). White is then in a position to luff Black to the wrong side of the mark and so gain the inside berth.

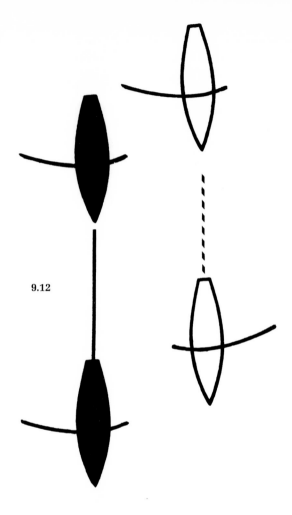

9.12

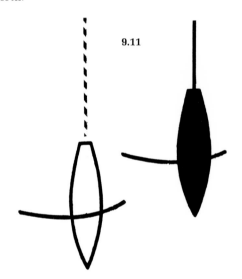

9.11

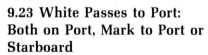

9.23 White Passes to Port: Both on Port, Mark to Port or Starboard

Mark to port

White decides to overtake to port since it offers the advantage of an inside berth at the next mark. However, she risks being luffed. To avoid this, White gybes onto starboard (9.12). She now has right of way and is entitled to sail in any

direction she likes, but she must give Black ample time and opportunity to keep clear.

Black will probably have to gybe in order to keep clear. Both are now on starboard tack, with Black to windward (9.13). Since Black is ahead of the mast abeam position White is not permitted to sail above the proper course to the next mark.

However, if they were initially on port tack it is quite likely that they had sailed over to the starboard side of the course, in which case they

9.13

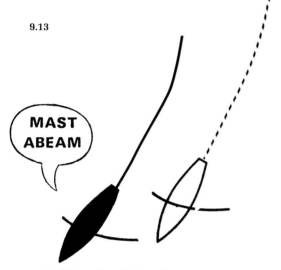

MAST
ABEAM

are probably sailing below the proper course to the downwind mark. In such circumstances (9.14) White is allowed to harden up to that

proper course, but not above it, and Black is obliged to do so since she is sailing below her proper course (Rule 39). If they have to luff up far, then Black might break White's overlap. Otherwise, White has an overlap and thus right to water when they arrive at the mark.

Rather than lose the overlap, White may actually be sailing fast enough to increase it until she is ahead of Black (9.15). White still does not have luffing rights, but she may regain them by gybing twice. White then ends up back on starboard, but with a new overlap (by virtue of her gybes – Rule 38.3) and so now has luffing rights. This is fairly easy to do on a sailboard, especially in light winds, even when on a broad reach rather than a dead run. Black is then in the position described for White in Section 9.22.

On a port-hand course, White can now sail straight for the mark, luffing and bearing away as she pleases, and then gybe round it comfortably in the lead.

9.14

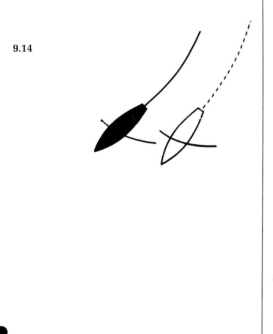

9.15

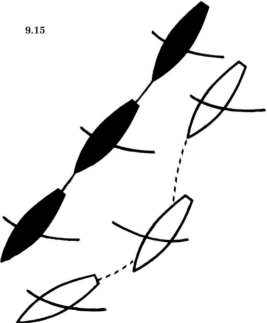

Mark to starboard

The position described at the beginning of this Section may also occur as the boards converge for a starboard-hand mark. White is unlikely to choose to pass to port when it is a starboard-hand course since it offers no advantages to do so. Should she find herself in this position, her tactics are identical to those for a port-hand course.

When she has regained luffing rights on starboard, as shown above, she is then in a position to luff Black as necessary to gain the inside, rather than the outside, berth at the leeward mark. This is described fully in the next Chapter.

9.24 White Passes to Starboard: Both on Port Tack, Mark to Port

This position offers no real advantages to White on a port-hand course. However, it may arise when two boards converge for the leeward mark.

White has two alternatives. She may decide to slow down and cross Black's stern (9.16) to try to pass her on the other side – a much more favourable position described in Section 9.23 previously. Alternatively, she may persist with passing on Black's starboard side.

While White continues on her port tack Black is free to sail directly for the mark, or above her course. She is not, of course, allowed to bear down on White. She may also gybe onto starboard at any time to gain right of way, although she must give White time to keep clear. If both boards gybe then Black has luffing rights until White attains the mast abeam position. If she wished she could do this immediately, force White to gybe too, and then luff her. However, if she did then White would probably back out of the luff and cross Black's stern to pass her to port, thus putting Black in a worse position.

White continues on port tack until she is ahead of the mast abeam position. She then gybes twice to gain luffing rights, with the intention of luffing Black so as to gain the inside

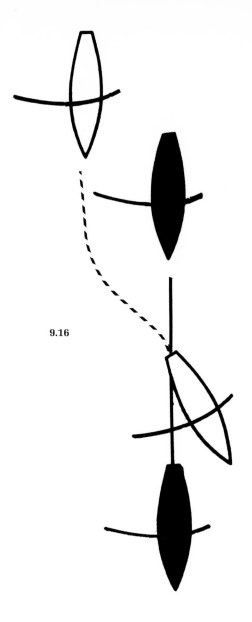

9.16

berth at the mark (9.17). Instead of gybing immediately, Black here allows White to continue passing on her starboard side and deals with the situations as they arise.

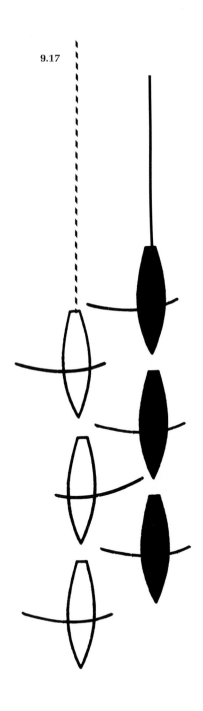

9.17

Black can easily counter White's actions by herself gybing onto starboard (9.18). Black can then sail White in any direction she pleases.

White gybes again so she is now on the same tack as Black, and if she is far enough ahead she calls 'Mast abeam', forcing Black to sail directly to the mark (9.19).

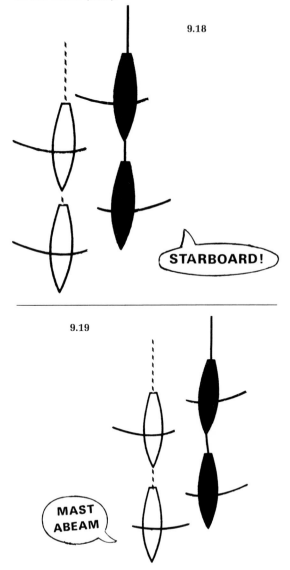

9.18

STARBOARD!

9.19

MAST ABEAM

Black is obliged to sail no higher than the direct course to the next mark (9.20). If at all possible she stays on starboard tack, even sailing slightly by the lee, since there is then nothing that White can do to gain the inside overlap for the mark. White also tries to remain on starboard tack if at all possible (9.20). However, she may be unable to and will have to gybe before Black does.

Black has managed to stay on starboard and now finds herself with right of way again (9.21). She hardens up, since the farther she can sail White past the mark the more difficult it will be for her to eventually gain that inside berth.

Of course White immediately gybes again. It is now a new overlap, and to stop Black from

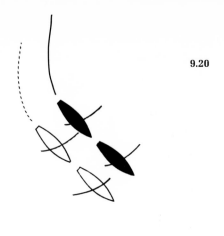

9.20

luffing White has to claim 'Mast abeam' once again. Until then, Black is entitled to continue luffing.

Black bears away once again (9.22). This time they are far enough past the mark that Black can safely claim a mast abeam position. White is then prevented from luffing her and so Black will safely reach the mark in the lead.

Had Black initially gybed onto port tack before White did (9.23) and had she then been unable to claim 'Mast abeam', then White would be in a position to gybe and luff Black (9.24) and so to try to gain the inside berth at the mark (see Chapter 10).

9.21

STARBOARD!

MAST ABEAM

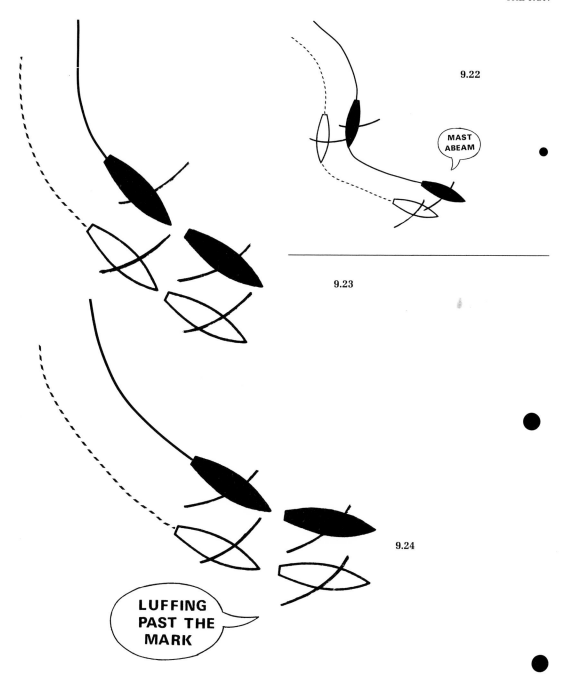

9.22

9.23

9.24

9.25 White Passes to Starboard: Both on Port, Mark to Starboard

White may pass either close to Black or at a distance from her. If she passes close to Black, then Black quickly gybes and calls 'Starboard' while luffing slowly (9.25).

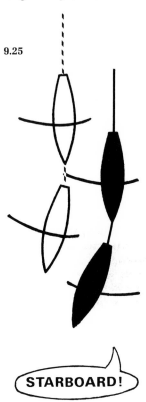

9.25

White responds by gybing to keep clear (9.26). Black may then luff as quickly as she likes in order to prevent White from establishing an overlap that will give her water at the mark.

On the other hand, if White attacks from a greater distance then there is less danger of this happening (9.27). This time Black cannot use the same tactic. She gybes, as before, but this time does not luff up so violently. Instead she sails a line that will take her over towards the port side of the course, but without sailing so high that White will be able to call 'Mast abeam'.

White again gybes to keep clear. The problem

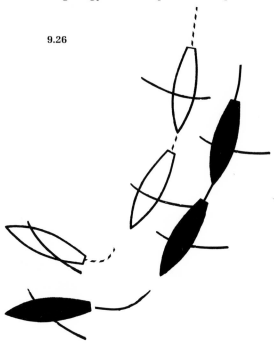

9.26

is that unless White can curtail Black's luff, then Black will continue sailing her off to the wrong side of the course until Black is sure that she can beat White to the mark. White must break Black's luff, and this can only be done by sailing faster until she can eventually call 'Mast abeam'.

Once White has achieved this and called 'Mast abeam' Black must bear away for the mark and will probably have to gybe (9.28). It may be that Black has managed to sail White far enough and so when they bear away Black breaks the overlap and goes on to round first. Black's defence has then been successful.

On the other hand, if White manages to curtail Black's luff early enough she may be able to keep her overlap (9.29). White then rounds first and her attack has been successful.

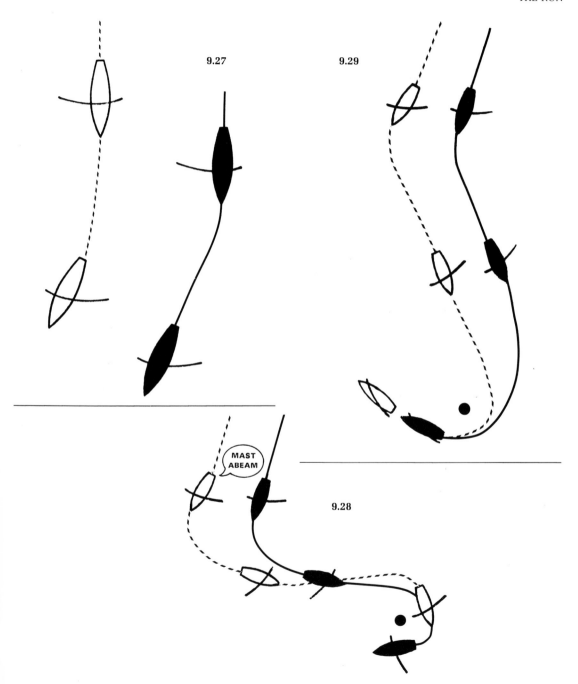

9.27

9.29

9.28

129

9.26 White Passes to Starboard: Both on Starboard, Mark to Starboard

This position is essentially the same as that described in Section 9.25. Black defends herself by luffing either slowly or quickly depending on how close White is.

9.27 White Passes to Port: Both on Starboard, Mark to Starboard

Black has no defence since she cannot bear down on White, nor can she acquire rights by gybing since she would then be on port tack.

White sails fast until she is ahead of the mast abeam position as seen by Black (9.30). She then gybes twice and gains luffing rights. White is then in a position to try to gain the inside berth by luffing Black over to the wrong side (see Chapter 10).

9.3 SAILING IN A GROUP

9.31 White Leads

As previously mentioned, it is not easy to defend a lead on the run since the attacking boards are upwind and have clearer air. To keep her lead White has to stay in undisturbed wind.

As White rounds the windward mark, therefore, she gybes and sails off on port tack towards the starboard side of the course (9.31–2). She can then stay clear of most of the wind shadows from her opponents.

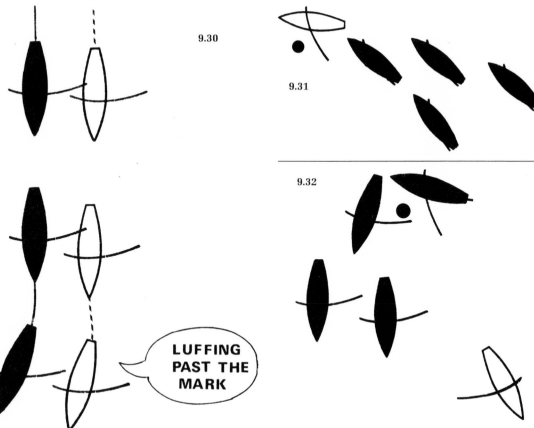

9.30

9.31

9.32

LUFFING PAST THE MARK

Furthermore, later on in the run she will have to gybe in order to sail for the leeward mark. She will then be rejoining the fleet when she is on starboard tack with right of way, and will also be approaching from the correct side to obtain an inside overlap at the mark and so maintain her lead even if some of the other boards have actually caught up with her (9.33).

Alternatively, she could have sailed over to the port side of the course, but though she might find clear wind over there she would then have to approach the mark from the outside and on port tack.

As at all times, she must remember to concentrate on sailing fast, and not on how fast everyone else is sailing!

9.32 White in the Middle or Back of the Group

Again White must keep clear of the wind shadows of anyone behind her. However, she is also in a position to use her own shadow to slow down boards that are ahead. Her tactics are to follow the leaders after rounding the windward mark, keeping her own air clear with minor course changes when necessary, while blanketing an opponent whenever the opportunity presents itself. In this way White will gradually catch up and overtake opponents one by one, as described earlier in this Chapter. Deciding which side to pass them on depends on whether the leeward mark is to be left to port or starboard, and on whether there are any other

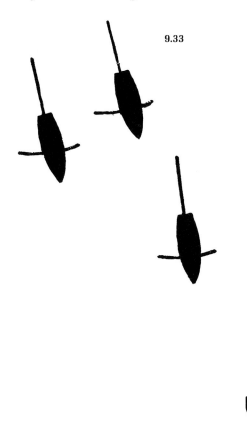

9.33

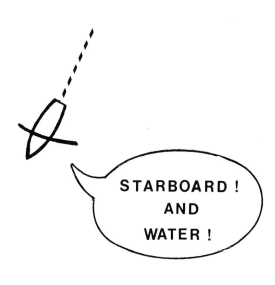

STARBOARD! AND WATER!

boards nearby. If the mark is to be left to port it is nearly always preferable to pass other boards to port, for reasons that have been discussed in Sections 9.21 to 9.24.

If the mark is to be left to starboard the problem is more difficult. If White is certain that she will overtake the board ahead of her and be clear ahead by the time they reach the leeward mark, then it is probably safer to overtake on the port side, thus avoiding the risk of being luffed. On the other hand, if they are near the mark White will be more concerned with gaining the inside berth, and water for the mark, and so may

decide to pass to starboard. Again the tactics are as already described.

It is worth noting, however, that the nearby presence of other boards can be used to enable White to overtake her opponent more easily. In (9.34), for example, Black is overlapping Grey without luffing rights. White decides to overtake Black to windward. Black is prevented from luffing White since she must have luffing rights over Grey as well as White in order to do so (Rule 38.6). Knowing she is safe from interference, White passes between Black and Grey. This tactic may also be used when all are on port tack.

9.34

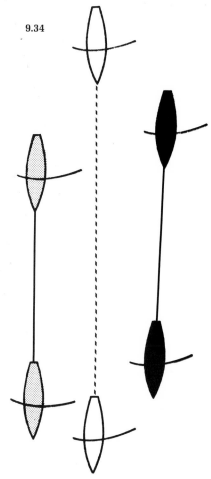

10

The Leeward Mark, from a Run

10.1 ROUNDING ALONE

As with rounding the downwind mark from a reach, it is important to start the turn well before reaching the mark.

If White apppoaches a port-hand mark on port tack, or a starboard-hand mark on starboard, then she will not have to gybe to round it. In such a case (10.1) she approaches wide and starts to turn early, passing near the mark only when she is already closehauled, and so losing little distance to windward (see also Section 8.1)

If White approaches on the opposite tack to that described above, then she will have to gybe in order to round (10.2). In light winds this may be done while still on a run, well before the mark, and then it can be rounded as described above.

10.2

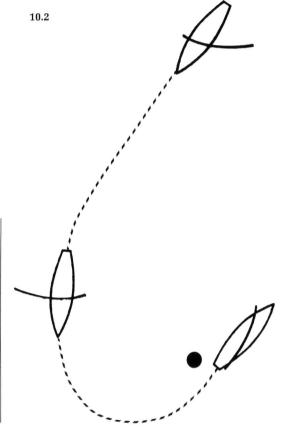

10.1

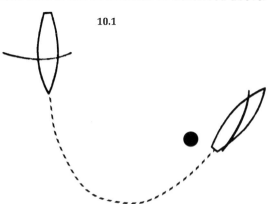

However, this is not possible in stronger winds and instead the gybe is included in the turn (10.3). Again the mark is approached wide, and when about level with it White does a quick flare gybe, luffing up when she comes out of the gybe so that by the time she pulls the sail in and

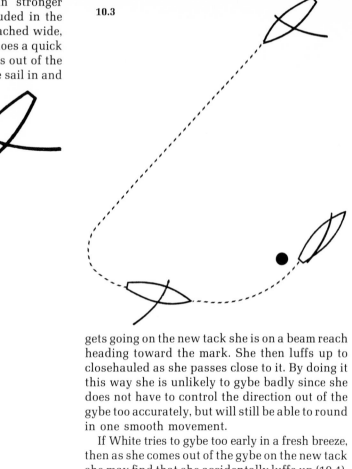

10.3

10.4

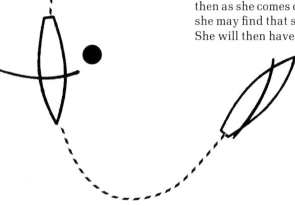

gets going on the new tack she is on a beam reach heading toward the mark. She then luffs up to closehauled as she passes close to it. By doing it this way she is unlikely to gybe badly since she does not have to control the direction out of the gybe too accurately, but will still be able to round in one smooth movement.

If White tries to gybe too early in a fresh breeze, then as she comes out of the gybe on the new tack she may find that she accidentally luffs up (10.4). She will then have to bear away sharply in order to leave the mark on the correct side (not easy in a blow) and will inevitably pass too close to it to round well.

On leaving the mark it is best not to tack immediately, but rather to get up speed on a closehauled course first and then tack at leisure.

10.2 ROUNDING WITH ONE OPPONENT

10.21 White to Port:
Both on Starboard, Mark to Port

White has the inside berth and merely sails towards the mark until she can round it, concentrating on rounding well as discussed above (10.5). If Black is able to gybe across White's bow while keeping clear of her, she does so.

If not, she tries to persuade White to pass too close to the mark so that she rounds badly (10.6). Black does this by asking White to sail for the mark and to stop luffing her (assuming that White does not have luffing rights). White, of course, is entitled to take as much room as she needs to make a good rounding. As White then rounds badly, Black gybes across her stern and sails through the gap onto White's windward quarter.

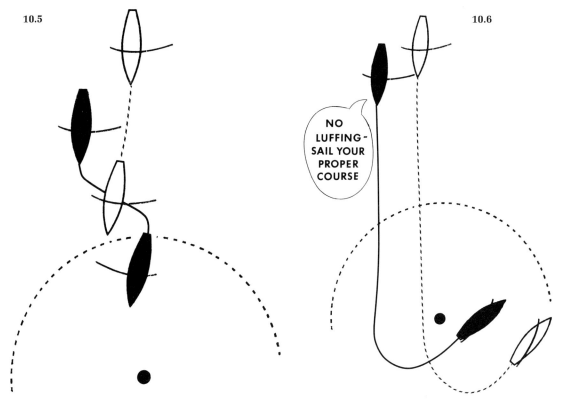

135

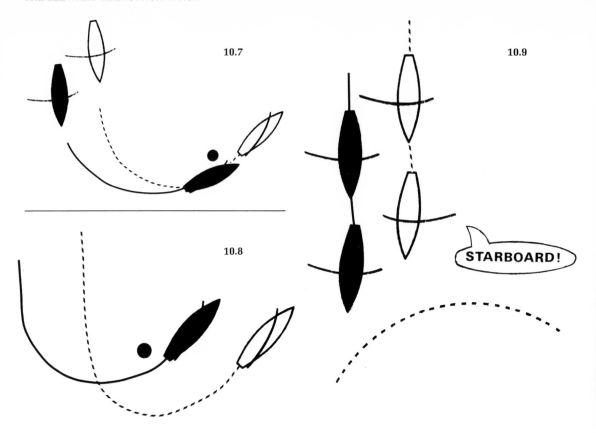

10.7

10.9

10.8

STARBOARD!

10.22 White to Port:
Both on Port, Mark to Port

Black may or may not have luffing rights. If she does not, then White has a guaranteed inside berth and merely sails for the mark, making sure that she rounds well (10.7). Black can only wait and hope for White to round badly, leaving a gap that she could slip through (10.8).

However, if Black does have luffing rights then White should immediately gybe onto starboard in order to gain right of way (10.9). The position then becomes that described immediately above and White rounds first.

If she does have luffing rights, Black must try to luff White past the mark (10.10). If White gybes then of course the tactic will have to be abandoned. However, if White does not gybe right away she may find that she has been luffed slightly and being on a broad reach can no longer gybe. In such a case White cannot defend herself from Black's luff until she can call 'Mast abeam', by which time Black may well have taken her past the wrong side of the mark.

If Black manages to luff her up to a broad reach White will be unable to gybe, especially in a strong wind, and so Black will be able to carry on luffing her past the mark until eventually she can gybe back to round it in the lead (10.11). On returning to the mark from the wrong side, White is not allowed to prevent Black from gybing round it, even though White is on starboard tack (Rule 42.2a).

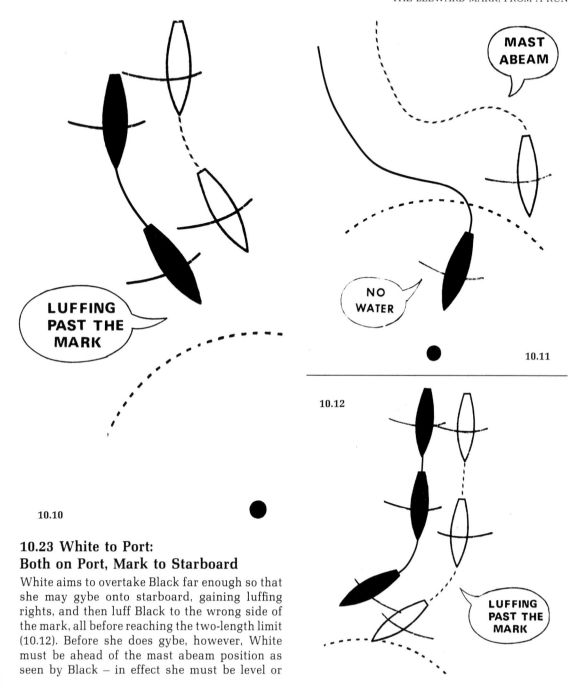

10.10

10.11

10.12

10.23 White to Port: Both on Port, Mark to Starboard

White aims to overtake Black far enough so that she may gybe onto starboard, gaining luffing rights, and then luff Black to the wrong side of the mark, all before reaching the two-length limit (10.12). Before she does gybe, however, White must be ahead of the mast abeam position as seen by Black – in effect she must be level or

137

10.13

10.14

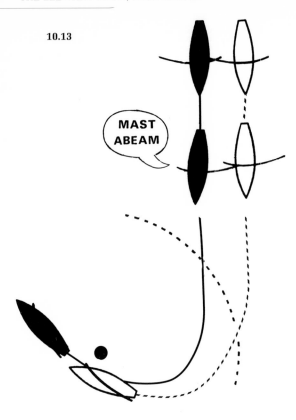

ahead of Black. Until that point she must be content with the outside berth.

Black's defence is to keep herself ahead of the mast abeam position (10.13). Then if White gybes she also gybes, and snuffs out any ideas of a luff with a quick call of 'Mast abeam'. Black then keeps her inside berth, and must round perfectly, leaving no gaps for White to slip through.

Once White has taken Black past the mark (see diagram 10.12) she gybes again to round it first (10.14).

Alternatively, Black may luff White just enough to stop her from being able to gybe (10.15).

If White finds that she is unable to gybe she must try to gain a mast abeam position and curtail Black's luff as soon as possible (10.16). Once she has stopped the luff she may still have time to gybe and luff Black in return.

However, if Black can keep White from gybing until near the two-length limit she can then sail for the mark and legalize her inside berth.

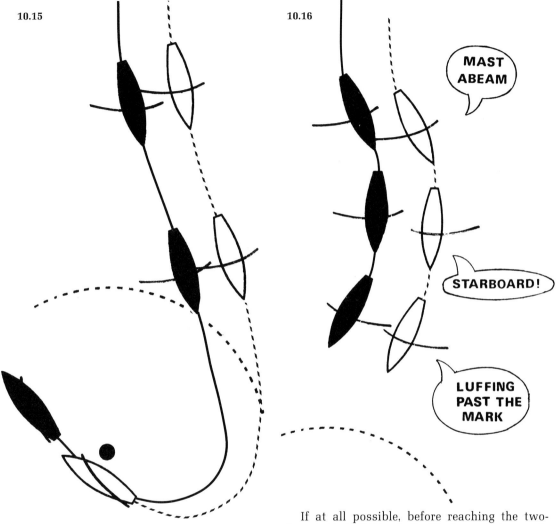

10.15

10.16

MAST ABEAM

STARBOARD!

LUFFING PAST THE MARK

10.24 White to Port:
Both on Starboard, Mark to Starboard

Black has a safe position unless White has, or gains, luffing rights before the two-length limit. Black concentrates on rounding well, making sure that she loses no distance to windward.

If at all possible, before reaching the two-length limit White luffs Black past the mark, calling out her intentions (10.17). If she has just overtaken Black, White may obtain luffing rights by putting in two quick gybes, as shown here.

If White is not far enough ahead to gain luffing rights she encourages Black to round badly by giving her the minimum amount of room, and then sails through the gap that she leaves to get onto Black's windward quarter (10.18).

10.17

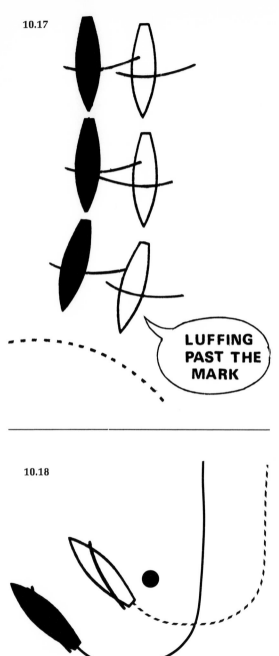

LUFFING PAST THE MARK

10.18

10.19

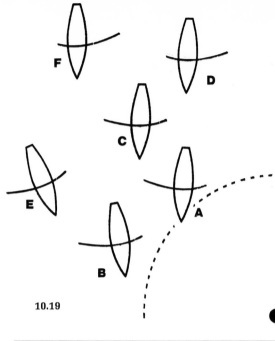

10.20

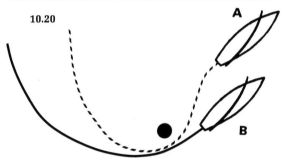

10.3 ROUNDING IN A GROUP

Once within the two-length limit, the Port – Starboard Rule 36 no longer applies, and so the following is equally valid for a leeward mark that is to be left to starboard (10.19).

A has the inside berth and arrives first at the mark. She concentrates on rounding well (10.20). As she comes out of the mark she luffs up slightly to force B to go below her, and so takes the lead.

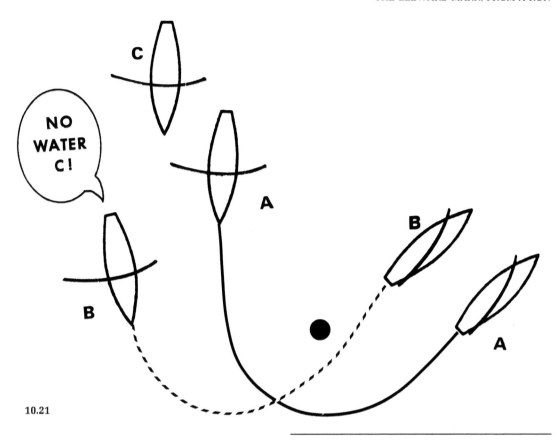

10.21

B calls out 'No water except A' and then makes sure that she rounds perfectly, preventing C from barging in (10.21). Should A round badly, B can sail through to the lead.

C Having been denied entry by B, C rounds as well as she can. Unfortunately, because she has to give way to both A and B she will probably end up to leeward of them both. To counter this she would normally slow down and then follow close on B's stern. However, in this case she cannot do that since she is obliged to give D water and so ends up to leeward of her instead (10.22).

D claims water on C. She is sufficiently far behind B and A that she can concentrate on rounding well without having to give way to

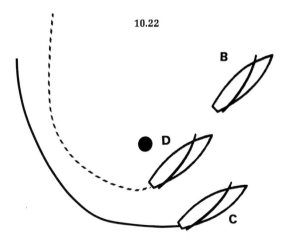

10.22

141

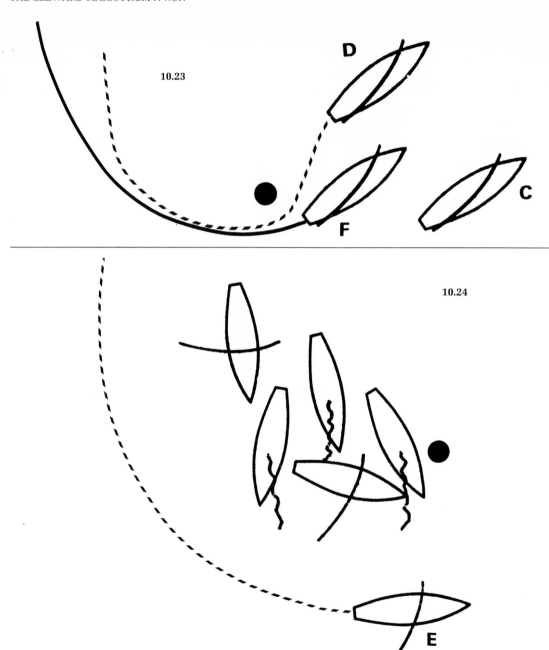

10.23

D

F

C

10.24

E

anyone. She will in fact end up only just behind B (10.22). As she comes out of the mark she also luffs up, like A, to keep to windward of F who will be following her (10.23).

E has to give water to all the above. She shouts 'No water, F' but is unlikely to be able to enforce that. She cannot slow down to cross their sterns, since she would then have to let F go through as well. Instead she rounds outside the whole group, staying in clean air as much as she can and avoiding the collisions and confusion that often result in a raft of boards stuck on the mark (10.24). In light winds, with large fleets, and particularly with a stream flowing against the wind, there will frequently be a mass of boards at the mark all struggling to round it in no wind and colliding with each other, with the result that none of them get round. In such circumstances E may well find that she comes out of the mark ahead, leaving all the confusion behind.

10.25

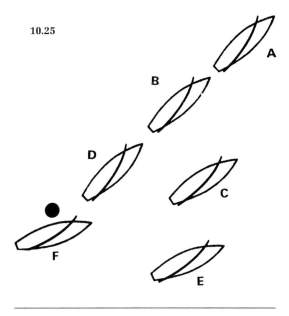

10.26

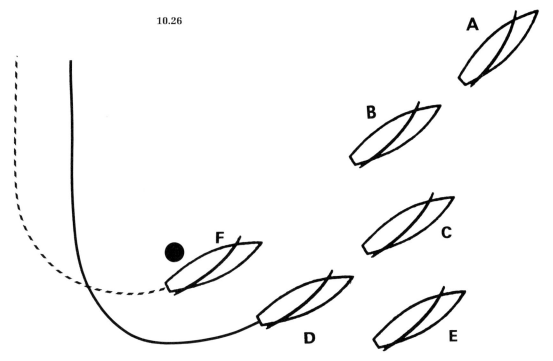

However, in moderate winds and with few boards, as shown in diagram 10.25, E will fare very badly.

F Although last in the group, F has freedom of movement and is able to round perfectly, following close on D's stern (10.25). As with B, if D rounds poorly then F can slip through to third place on the next leg (10.26).

From this analysis the value of an inside berth is easily seen. In particular, it is instructive to note how well F did, simply because she had to give way to no one. Also, although in this case E did badly it is worth remembering to look ahead to see whether a raft of boards has formed, and if it has to sail right around the whole lot.

Finally, it is also important to remember the direction of the stream. If it is flowing with the wind, some boards may be carried downwind (downstream) of the mark and so there will often be gaps through which one can sail by starting to turn early enough (10.27). On the other hand, if the tide is flowing against the wind (10.28) then any boards that start rounding at the normal distance from the mark will be swept onto it, resulting in the rafts mentioned above.

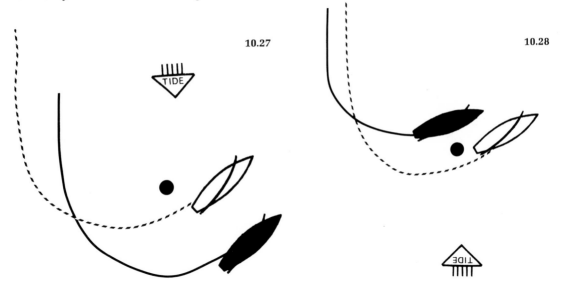

10.27

10.28

11
The Finish

11.1 FINISH TO WINDWARD

11.11 Which End of the Line?

In Chapter 2 we decided that one end of the start line is usually more favourable than the other by virtue of the fact that it is farther upwind and thus nearer to the windward mark. If, say, the port end of the start line is favoured for starting, since it is closer to the windward mark, then it is also true that, *for that same line*, the starboard end must be closer to the leeward mark. Therefore if the same line is used for both start and finish, as shown in diagram 11.1, you will finish sooner by heading for the starboard end than the port end.

So, on starting the last beat the first thing to decide is which end of the line to head for. Often, by the end of the final beat the finishing order will be clearly apparent with minutes between successive boards. Just as frequently, however, two or more may finish almost simultaneously. It is in these situations that the sailor who has chosen the correct end of the line to finish at is the one who wins. In diagram 11.2 the line is biased for a port-end start – that is, a starboard-end finish. White has just given way to Black by crossing behind her stern, and yet by the time White has finished Black is still two lengths away from the line!

So choosing the right end can win races. How

to do it? Well, the criteria are exactly the same as for the start line – except of course that we then choose the opposite end. But we cannot sail up and down the finish line in the middle of a race to decide which end to go for, so we have to resort

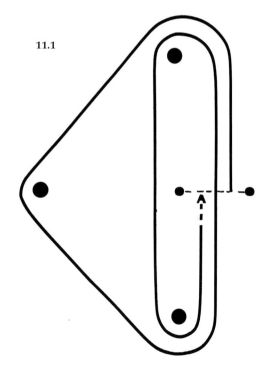

11.1

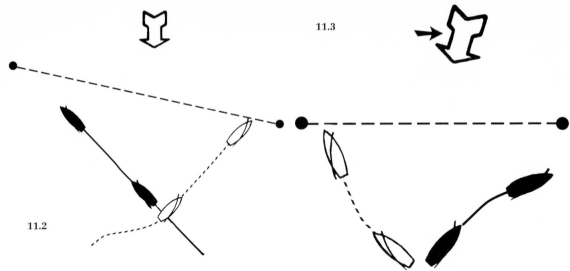

11.3

11.2

to more difficult (and unfortunately less accurate) methods.

When the start line is in such a position that it can also be used for the finish, we already know which end is favoured although allowance must be made for any significant change in wind direction. For example, if the wind veers during the race then the port end of the line will become progressively more favoured (11.3).

Usually, however, the race is started at the leeward mark and the finish line is laid at the windward mark during the race. When this is the case, or indeed, whenever the line is laid during the race, then it should be examined at any time that we sail near it during the race. If the line is laid immediately after the start it will be crossed, or at least approached, on every lap

and the favoured end should be determined every time so that by the end of the race we have a fairly good idea of which end to go for.

There are no easy ways to do this. If we actually pass through the line we can try to estimate whether we cross it at an angle greater or less than $45°$. Here White is on the second beat and passes through the line (11.4). By comparing the angles at which she and Black each cross it she decides that she is crossing at less than $45°$ while Black is at an angle greater than $45°$. Since White is on starboard tack this means that the port end must be farther upwind, and so the starboard end is favoured for finishing. On the next beat she checks it again, and so on the final beat she is fairly certain that the starboard end is the correct one to go for.

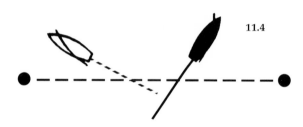

11.4

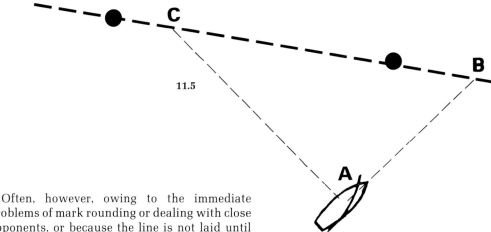

11.5

Often, however, owing to the immediate problems of mark rounding or dealing with close opponents, or because the line is not laid until the last lap, it is impossible to study it before approaching on the final beat. This makes it much more difficult. As White approaches the line (11.5), preferably from the middle rather than one side of the course, she tries to estimate just where the line lies, and then whether the distance to it (or its extension) straight ahead (distance AB) is greater or less than the distance to the line at right angles to her (distance AC). If AB is the shorter distance then the port end is favoured. If AC is shorter the starboard end is favoured. Of course this needs to be checked and rechecked a number of times as the line is approached, since it is extremely difficult to judge accurately until one is very close.

Any boards that are finishing ahead of White may help her to choose the right end. Particularly useful are two boards that are obviously level with each other but go for opposite ends of the line. Whichever one finishes first is presumably at the favoured end, assuming they both sailed at about the same speed. White watches Grey and Black carefully (11.6). Since Black wins, White sails for the same starboard end of the line.

Trying to determine the correct end to finish at should be practised at every opportunity, even when you are miles from the nearest opponent, since sometime it will prove vital and all the practice will then pay dividends.

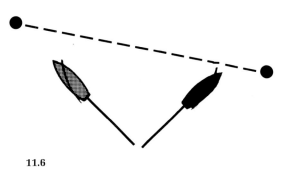

11.6

147

11.12 Beating an Opponent to the Line

11.121 Port end favoured

If White is clearly ahead of Black, then she merely covers Black to the finish as described in Chapter 3. If the line is heavily biased and Black persists in heading for the starboard end, then White may decide to break off her cover to finish at the port end just to make sure that any nearby opponents do not have the opportunity to slip through and finish ahead of both of them (11.7).

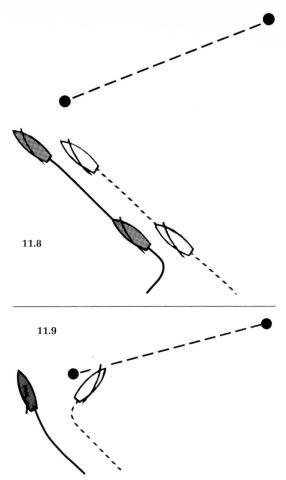

11.8

11.9

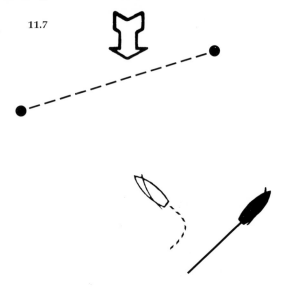

11.7

White therefore sails for the port end on starboard tack. She may find that Grey then tacks under her (11.8). If they can both lay the line, then Grey has an advantage over White since she is nearer the favoured end. To prevent this White approaches the line slightly below the lay line for the outer end. Now if Grey tacks underneath her White can sail her past the mark. This works even if Grey is actually ahead of White, as long as White can prevent Grey from tacking across her bow.

Once they are level with the mark White tacks at the last minute to finish first (11.9).

On the other hand Grey might decide to give way to White, intending to tack as soon as she

reaches the lay line (11.10). Thus Grey will be approaching the line on starboard and so will be able to stop White from tacking for the line.

To prevent this White tacks as Grey passes under her stern, taking care not to hit her should they both tack simultaneously (Rule 41.4). White can then either take Grey past the starboard end of the line, so finishing first, or she may tack for the port end. This has the disadvantage of loosing a board length during the tack, which may be enough to give Grey the lead even though she finishes at the wrong end.

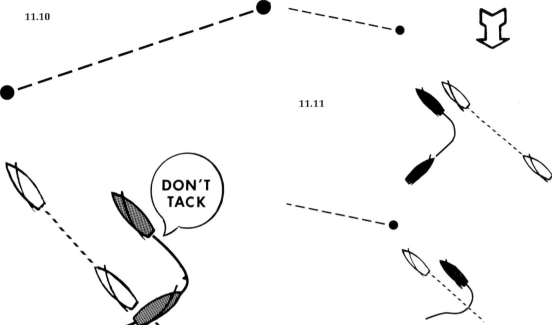

11.10

11.11

DON'T
TACK

11.122 Starboard end favoured

Again, tactics are aimed at being nearer to the favoured end of the finish line than our opponents. If there are a large number of closely bunched opponents then we must aim to cross the line right at the starboard end. Fortunately this is fairly easy. We simply sail to the lay line for the starboard end, tack onto starboard and sail to the finish. By approaching on starboard we have right of way over anyone trying to finish on port tack. For example (11.11), Black will either have to tack under White and so lose a length, and probably finish after her, or else bear away for her, overstand the mark and certainly finish second to her.

Tactics for a starboard-end finish are basically the same as for the windward mark on a starboard-hand course (see Section 4.12).

11.123 Photo finishes

White and Black are approaching the line and are clearly level with each other, neither being sure who will cross the line first (11.12). White realizes this, and so just before the line (about half a length away) she puts in a tack. The first part of a tack consists of luffing up to head-to-wind, and since this loses little speed White has in effect changed from sailing at about 45° to the line to sailing at right angles to it at much the same speed. So White sails a slightly shorter distance to the line (about 2–3ft) than Black, which may well make the difference between finishing first or second.

This tactic is very effective when used in such close finishes, but it must be timed correctly. Starting the tack too early will result not in crossing the line when still only head-to-wind, but rather in having to finish the turn and then continue sailing for the line on the new tack – having lost a good board length by tacking. So it is better to try it too late than too early. If it is used late then there is still some benefit in terms of distance gained from the luff, even though it is not as much as it might be: it may be just enough to win that particular encounter.

11.2 REACHING AND RUNNING FINISHES

11.21 Which End of the Line?

Finishing on a reach or a run is not as uncommon as starting off the wind. The most usual reason is that the race has been shortened, for one reason or another, to finish at either the wing mark or the leeward mark (whether from a reach or a run). In these circumstances the finish line is usually laid between the nominated mark and a committee boat carrying a blue flag. Normally the original course mark will be left to the correct side: on a port-hand course the committee boat will station herself at the starboard end of the line with the mark making the port end.

It should be remembered, however, that the committee boat may park herself at the other side of the mark. In such a case the correct course to the finish is to sail straight for the line, leaving the mark to the 'wrong' side rather than hooking round it – whatever the Sailing Instructions may say (11.13). The Racing Rules specifically prohibit a 'hook finish', in Part I – Definitions.

The favoured end of the line for finishing is normally the nearer one. It is not always that straightforward, however, and sometimes the closer end is not necessarily best.

On a close reach the windward mark may well be nearer than the leeward mark. Here the port end is nearer than the starboard end, but to get to it from the previous mark means sailing closehauled, as Black is doing (11.14). Rather than do that, White decides to free off slightly, sailing lower and so farther to the line but going much faster than Black and so finishing before her. Grey, however, rather overdoes it and sails off on a beam reach, not going much faster than White but with a greater distance to sail.

Another problem to be weighed up is that of sailing in dirty wind (11.15). This time it is the leeward end that is nearer, but Black (who has rounded the last mark in a group and set off for the leeward end) finds that she finishes after White, who rounded at the same time but went

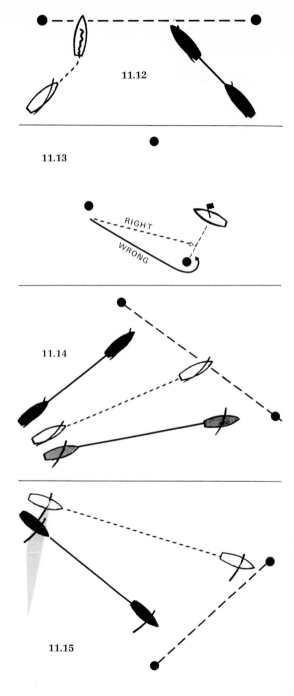

11.12

11.13

11.14

11.15

for the middle of the line, simply because White had clean air and so sailed faster, more than making up for the greater distance covered.

On a run, these problems are fewer and normally there are no reasons not to sail for the near end, since there will be problems finding clean air whichever end of the line is chosen.

SUMMARY

On a RUN Sail for the closer end.
On a *Windward end nearer*
REACH Sail for favoured end unless on
  a very close fetch, in which case
  sail fast and free for a point
  slightly farther down the line.
  Leeward end nearer
  Sail for a point as near to the
  leeward end as possible, but
  with clean air as the first
  priority.

11.22 Tactics

11.231 Windward end favoured

Tactics for finishing at the windward end of the line are directed against any opponents who might be to windward. Those below you cannot be attacked legitimately, and are also at a disadvantage because of the bais of the line.

Tactics against Black consist of luffing, either sharply, to gain a clear lead (11.16), or slowly, to push her past the mark (11.17).

The principles are similar to those for rounding a leeward mark (see Section 8.2) and the rules for water at the mark still apply, but it must be remembered that it is the board that crosses the line first that wins – not necessarily the one that gains the inside overlap.

11.232 Leeward end favoured

There are no really effective tactics for Black, who is to windward, but White may luff Black as necessary in order to keep her lead and she may even luff her past the windward mark to ensure that she wins. Otherwise, White just concentrates on sailing in clean air to the leeward end, while Black tries to sail over her (11.18).

11.233 On a run

Tactics are the same as for any run downwind. On rounding the final windward mark in a group, White will choose the side of the course that leads to the nearest end of the finish line (if she can tell which end that is from that distance) and concentrate on sailing fast in clean wind. If there is only one opponent, then White will use the tactics of Section 9.2 to stay ahead of her.

11.16

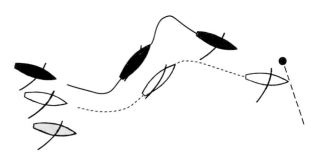

11.17

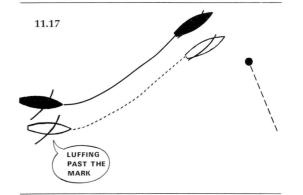

LUFFING PAST THE MARK

11.18

151

12
Other Competitions

Apart from triangle racing, there are a number of other forms of competition for sailboards. Most of them, such as Freestyle, Ins and Outs, and Slaloms, are contests of pure skill with little, if any, element of tactics involved. A few, such as Long Distance and 'round the island' races, do entail the use of tactics even though the course may consist almost entirely of broad-reaching. The tactics used are the same as those already described in this book, but there are a few idiosyncrasies.

Long Distance Races
These usually consist of sailing from one beach or island to another. The event may be staged over several days, such as the Grundig South Coast Marathon in England that covered over 100 miles in about a week. Often the course will consist of just one leg, whether it is a beat, a reach or a run, although the presence of headlands, harbour breakwaters or islands that need to be rounded may provide some variation. Whatever the actual course, the tactics will be the same as those discussed in the relevant chapters above. Needless to say, good mark rounding is not likely to be at a premium while stamina is.

Particular attention must be paid to the state of the tide and when it will change, since its correct interpretation will pay large dividends

over a five mile course. The weather forecast is also important, not just for deciding which sail to use but as an indication of wind shifts. The weather can change considerably during a day-long race, and as well as finding yourself with the wrong sail there may be a front coming that will turn the reach into a very long beat.

Finally, it is of course important to have well maintained, reliable equipment, extra warm and wind-proof clothing, and a reserve of strength and stamina for what may be a very gruelling test.

'Round the Island' Races
These are very popular since they are easy to organize and offer something different to the usual triangular courses. By its very nature such a race will include beating, reaching and running in various proportions. Also, one of the reaches will usually be in the island's wind shadow, unless it lies directly upwind of both the start and finish. Often the most important decision in the race is how close to the shore to sail this reach.

Here Black decides to sail close to the shore, taking the shortest distance (12.1). White sails very wide to avoid the wind shadow and so covers a much greater distance in stronger winds than Black. Grey is rather indecisive and so takes a middle course. Which of the three comes

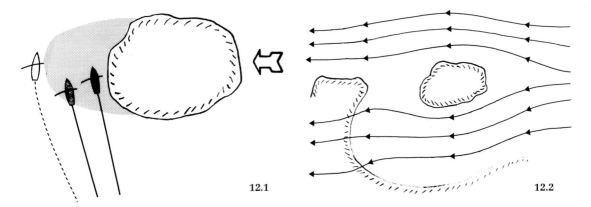

12.1

12.2

out first depends to a large extent on the conditions. In light airs White will almost certainly do best, since she keeps moving while the other two are becalmed. Black will probably beat Grey since neither has any wind, but Black has less distance to cover. In very strong winds with a low flat island there may be little difference in wind strength between them and so Black may come first, having the shortest distance to sail.

The island also affects the wind for the beat. As we saw earlier, wind tends to flow around rather than over obstructions, and in this case it produces a wind bend that favours sailing inshore. The reach across the windward side of the island, and the run, are both in clean air and tactics are the same as for any other race. However, the land topography may affect the wind to some degree, especially close to shore.

153

Appendix 1
Lee-bowing opponents

The terms 'lee bow' or 'lee-bowing' are used frequently. They refer to the particular situation where two boards are closehauled on the same tack with one positioned ahead and also on the leeward side of the other. Here, White is on Black's lee bow, and she is said to be lee-bowing Black. Because of the deflection of the wind by the leading board's sail, this position results in Black's sail being slightly backwinded by the air from White's sail. Black is slowed down, becomes unable to point so high to windward, and thus drops rapidly behind. For this trick to be effective, White must be as close to Black as possible and at least half a length ahead of her.

The term should not be confused with the situation where the tidal stream flowing against (i.e. onto) the leeward side of one's bow can be used to help make distance up to windward. This is often called 'lee-bowing the tide'.

Appendix 2
Circuit training on land

The training programme described here takes only fifteen minutes a day and needs no special equipment. The object of this training is to improve *endurance* (i.e. heart and lung performance) and also to strengthen the muscles used in windsurfing. To improve endurance the heart must be kept beating at a rate of more than 140 beats per minute (that is a pulse rate of more than 140) for at least 15 minutes, and this should be done at least three times a week. To measure your own pulse rate, place three fingers of one hand lightly on the inside of the other wrist, just below the base of the thumb. Having found the pulse count it for 15 seconds and multiply the figure by 4 for the pulse rate per minute. Before starting the exercises it is important that you should see your doctor if you have any doubt about your health, particularly your heart.

The programme consists of six exercises which make up one circuit. The number of repetitions to be done of each exercise is shown on the left, increasing through four steps for greater difficulty. Start with the lowest number of repetitions. Do three complete circuits as fast as you can, paying attention to good technique and to correct breathing, and at the end time your pulse rate. If it is above 180/min. then you must slow down slightly next time. (The heart beats less efficiently at such a speed, and so it can be dangerous.) If you did the circuits in less

than 15 minutes, then next time do the second level of repetitions. If it took you more than 15 minutes but your pulse rate was below 140/min. then you need to work faster to get any benefit.

Continue doing three circuits at one level of repetitions until you can do them in under 15 minutes, then step up to the next level of reps. Once you can do the hardest circuit in 15 minutes adding repetitions will merely increase the bulk of your muscles with little further improvement in strength. Instead you should change to a programme using additional equipment such as weights or a Multi-gym.

Do not attempt to over-exercise too quickly. Start with the easiest circuit and work your way up without skipping a stage. If at any time you experience any chest pain then you must stop and rest, and consult your doctor.

1 STEP-UPS
10–15–20–25. Use a kitchen chair. Step up onto the chair making sure that you stand up straight and then step down again. Count one for each step-up, do the required number, then change legs and do the same number again.

2 SIT-UPS
5–10–15–20. Lie flat on the floor, tucking feet under a rail or radiator if necessary. Clasp hands behind head and sit up, keeping legs straight.

155

Try to touch knees with nose and then lie back again. Breathe in on sitting up.

3 PRESS-UPS

5–10–15–20. Lie on the floor face down with hands under shoulders, palms on the floor. Press against the floor, pushing the body up while keeping the back straight and rigid. Do not sag in the middle. When arms are *straight*, lower yourself slowly down to the ground, making sure that thighs and nose touch the floor simultaneously. Do not rest on the floor but start the next press-up as soon as your nose touches. If you need a rest, take it when up with your arms locked straight. Breathe in going down, out when pushing up.

4 PULL-UPS

10–15–20–25. Use a strong table or desk that will not topple over, or alternatively use a stiff pole supported by two tables. The height should be such that you can only just reach it when lying underneath on your back. Grasp the pole or the edge of the table with your hands about shoulder

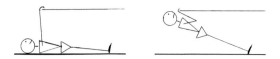

width apart. Pivoting on your heels with your back held straight and rigid, pull yourself up until your nose touches the table or pole and then lower yourself slowly back down to the floor. Breathe in going up, and out going down.

5 SQUAT THRUSTS

5–10–15–20. From a standing position, drop down to a squat with knees bent, back straight and hands palm down on the floor at the sides. Then, putting your weight on your hands, thrust your legs out backwards to the same straight position as at the top of a press-up. Pull them back into the squat position and then jump up, off the ground, to land in the standing position.

6 SIDE SWINGS

5–10–15–20. Stand with feet shoulder width apart, keeping your knees straight at all times. Bend forward to touch the ground with both hands, then swing arms sideways and up over your head, arching back and looking up at the ceiling as you do so. Carry on swinging your arms down to the other side to touch the floor once again. Count as you touch the floor, and then repeat in the opposite direction. Breathe in when going up, out on going down.

This programme can also be supplemented with jogging and stretching exercises.

Appendix 3

An example programme for an Olympic aspirant

This is the type of training programme that someone of top club racing standard might set for himself if he has ambitions of competing up to Olympic Games level. It is intended as a guide to the sort of programme that you should work out for yourself, depending on your final goal.

Year 1 Sail all the major open meetings and as many of the smaller ones as possible. Enter the National Championships of several classes of sailboard and finish in the top ten.

Winter training at home.

Year 2 Similar to last year, but also travelling abroad to enter the major National and International events. Finish in the top two or three at the home Nationals.

Winter training at home, with some International events if possible.

Year 3 Extensive worldwide competition, finishing in top five at International events.

Winter training abroad, e.g. Australia. Compete in all major events in the winter training country, and other major International events.

Year 4 Return home almost at peak performance. Sail the Olympic trials and win. Continue as for previous year, bringing skill and fitness up to their peak.

Sail Olympics and win the Gold medal.

[WIN]DSURFING RACING [TEC]HNIQUE
[Phill]ip Pudenz and
[Karl] Messmer

[...o]f the world's top sailors analyse,
[...]n and demonstrate the techniques
[...]d for race winning – fast tacking
[g]ybing, speed, mark rounding,
[tu]rns, trapezing, sail/board trim,
[...] tactics and picking the best
[...]s.

[...]g courses, signals, scoring, protests
[...]e racing rules particular to
[s]urfing are all covered, so getting
[...]d in racing, or improving your
[...], are made easier.
[...]s of colour and black/white photos
[se]quences by Michael Garff make
[u]nique book.
[...]ack, 180 pages

[HEA]VY WEATHER
[WIN]DSURFING
[F]unboards and Sinkers

[J]en Hönscheid and
[...] Winner

[In]ternational sailors explain and
[ill]ustrate how to handle strong
[...] high waves and surf. The many
[re]cent colour and monochrome
[...] photos and detailed text cover
[...]aspect of funboard and sinker
[...] equipment and tuning.
[...]-wind sailing demands a far wider
[...knowl]edge of wave and wind conditions,
[i]n breakers, and advanced
[techni]que. These are all covered, as
[...]including how to master carved
[f]ast gybing and tacking, sinker
[...] jumping and wave-riding. The
[...]s on competition are particularly
[...]gh and cover surf courses, slalom,
[...]e winning sailing techniques,
[...]y and tactics for every leg of
[...]lar course racing.
[...]ack, 120 pages

101 FREESTYLE WINDSURFING TRICKS
Sigi Hofmann

Starting with preparatory exercises,
and using series photography and a
breakdown of each trick into its
component moves, this book makes it
possible to begin with the easier ones
and work up to the most daring and
spectacular. The stunts here are graded
according to difficulty and wind strength,
and arranged in a logical sequence so
that you build on the techniques already
learned.
With many good tips on competition and
building a freestyle programme, by one
of the top international sailors.
Paperback, 120 pages

FASTER BETTER WINDSURFING
Uwe Preuss, Jochen Taaks and Sepp Winbeck

The latest methods for faster learning,
using correct sailing techniques from the
very start so that you improve faster and
get a sound basis for funboard and
advanced sailing. Based on the highly
successful teaching system of the
German Association of Windsurfing
Schools (VDWS).
Photo sequences help explain basic and
advanced tacking and gybing, trapeze
techniques, carved turns, beach and
water starts. The text also covers
essential background on equipment,
racing, collision avoidance and rights-
of-way, tides and currents, rescue and
emergency repairs.
Paperback, 122 pages

WINDSURFING TECHNIQUE
Niko Stickl and Michael Garff

A unique approach, using photomontage
and sequence pictures, with plenty of
spectacular colour shots of world-class
sailors in action. Starting from the basic
stance and manoeuvres, and with
detailed analysis and instruction taking
you up to advanced sailing techniques,
this is the book for improving your
performance.
Hardback, 180 pages

SAILBOARDS CUSTOM-MADE
Hans Fichtner and Michael Garff

Do-it-yourself sailboard building is a
practical, economical way of having
a fun board, for the kids to learn on, or to
try out your own ideas. Hans Fichtner is
a shaper for Mistral and here describes
the methods and tools that are most
suitable for amateur builders and will
give a satisfying, quality result.
8 pages of colour board graphics.
Paperback, 120 pages

Second Edition in preparation

Available through booksellers and some
windsurfing shops, or in case of difficulty write
to the Marketing Dept.

STANFORD MARITIME
Member Company of the George Philip Group
12 Long Acre, London WC2E 9LP, U.K.